Assessment Guide
Module J

HOLT McDOUGAL

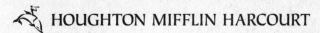

HOUGHTON MIFFLIN HARCOURT

Acknowledgements for Covers

Cover Photo Credits

Fiber-optic cable (bg) ©Dennis O'Clair/Stone/Getty Images; *pacific wheel* (l) ©Geoffrey George/Getty Images; *snowboarder* (cl) ©Jonathan Nourok/Photographer's Choice/Getty Images; *water droplet* (cr) ©L. Clarke/Corbis; *molecular structure* (r) ©Stockbyte/Getty Images

Printed in the U.S.A.

ISBN 978-0-547-59349-4

3 4 5 6 7 8 9 10   0982   20 19 18 17 16 15 14 13 12
4500357085   A B C D E F G

Contents

Unit 2 Sound

Unit 3 Light

End-of-Module Test

Answer Sheet

Answer Key

INTRODUCTION

Overview

ScienceFusion provides parallel instructional paths for teaching important science content. You may choose to use the print path, the digital path, or a combination of the two. The quizzes, tests, and other resources in this Assessment Guide may be used with either path.

The *ScienceFusion* assessment options are intended to give you maximum flexibility in assessing what your students know and what they can do. The program's formative and summative assessment categories reflect the understanding that assessment is a learning opportunity for students, and that students must periodically demonstrate mastery of content in cumulative tests.

All *ScienceFusion* tests are available—and editable—in ExamView and online at thinkcentral.com. You can customize a quiz or test for your classroom in many ways:

- adding or deleting items
- adjusting for cognitive complexity, Bloom's taxonomy level, or other measures of difficulty
- changing the sequence of items
- changing the item formats
- editing the question itself

All of these changes, except the last, can be made without invalidating the content correlation of the item.

This Assessment Guide is your directory to assessment in *ScienceFusion*. In it you'll find copymasters for Lesson Quizzes, Unit Tests, Unit Reviews, Performance-Based Assessments Alternative Assessments, and End-of-Module Tests; answers and explanations of answers; rubrics; a bubble-style answer sheet; and suggestions for assessing student progress using performance, portfolio, and other forms of integrated assessment.

You will also find additional assessment prompts and ideas throughout the program, as indicated on the chart that follows.

Assessment in *ScienceFusion* Program

	Student Editions	Teacher Edition	Assessment Guide	Digital Lessons	Online Resources at thinkcentral.com	ExamView Test Generator
Formative Assessment						
Assessing Prior Knowledge						
Engage Your Brain	X					
Unit Pretest			X		X	X
Embedded Assessment						
Active Reading Questions	X					
Interactivities	X					
Probing Questions		X				
Formative Assessment		X				
Classroom Discussions		X				
Common Misconceptions		X				
Learning Alerts		X				
Embedded Questions and Tasks				X		
Student Self-Assessments				X		
Digital Lesson Quiz				X		
When used primarily for teaching						
Lesson Review	X	X				
Lesson Quiz			X		X	X
Alternative Assessment			X		X	
Performance-Based Assessment			X			
Portfolio Assessment, guidelines			X			
Summative Assessment						
End of Lessons						
Visual Summary	X	X				
Lesson Quiz			X		X	X
Alternative Assessment		X	X		X	
Rubrics			X		X	
End of Units						
Unit Review	X		X		X	X
Answers		X	X		X	
Test Doctor Answer Explanations		X	X			X
Unit Test A (on level)			X		X	X
Unit Test B (below level)			X		X	X
End of Module						
End-of-Module Test			X		X	X

Formative Assessment

Assessing Prior Knowledge

Frequently in this program, you'll find suggestions for assessing what your students already know before they begin studying a new lesson. These activities help you warm up the class, focus minds, and activate students' prior knowledge.

In This Assessment Guide

Each of the units begins with a Unit Pretest consisting of multiple-choice questions that assess prior and prerequisite knowledge. Use the Pretest to get a snapshot of the class and help you organize your pre-teaching.

In the Student Edition

Engage Your Brain Simple, interactive warm-up tasks get students thinking, and remind them of what they may already know about the lesson topics.

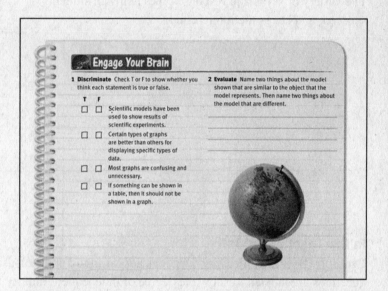

Active Reading Questions Students first see the lesson vocabulary on the opening page, where they are challenged to show what they know about the terms. Multiple exposures to the key terms throughout the lesson lead to mastery.

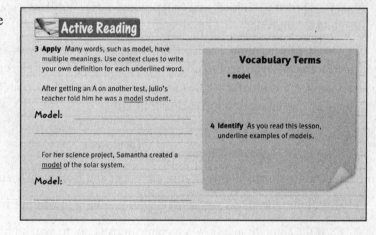

In the Teacher Edition

Opening Your Lesson At the start of each TE lesson Opening Your Lesson suggests questions and activities that help you assess prerequisite and prior knowledge.

Embedded Assessment

Once you're into the lesson, you'll continue to find suggestions, prompts, and resources for ongoing assessment.

Student Edition

Active Reading Questions and Interactivities Frequent questions and interactive prompts are embedded in the text, where they give students instant feedback on their comprehension. They ask students to respond in different ways, such as writing, drawing, and annotating the text. The variety of skills and response types helps all students succeed, and keeps them interested.

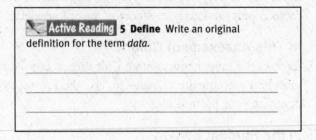

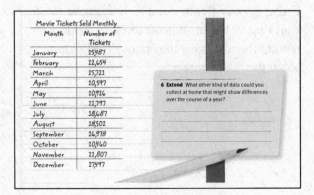

In the Teacher Edition

Probing Questions Probing questions appear in the point-of-use teaching suggestions. These questions are labeled to show the degree of independent inquiry they require. The three levels of inquiry—Directed, Guided, and Independent—give students experience that builds toward independent analysis.

Classroom Discussions Discussion is a natural opportunity to gauge how well students have absorbed the material, and to assess any misconceptions or gaps in their understanding. Students also learn from each other in this informal exchange. Classroom discussion ideas appear throughout the lesson in the Teacher Edition.

Tips for Classroom Discussions

- Allow students plenty of time to reflect and formulate their answers.

- Call upon students you sense have something to add but who haven't spoken.

- At the same time, allow reluctant students not to speak unless they choose to.

- Encourage students to respond to each other as well as to you.

Misconceptions and Learning Alerts The Teacher Background pages at the start of a unit describe common misconceptions and identify the lessons in which the misconceptions can be addressed. Strategies for addressing the misconceptions appear in the point-of-use teaching notes. Additional Learning Alerts help you introduce and assess challenging topics.

Formative Assessment A final formative assessment strategy appears on the Evaluate page at the end of each lesson, followed by reteaching ideas.

In This Assessment Guide

Several of the assessment strategies described in this book can be used either as formative or as summative instruments, depending on whether you use them primarily for teaching or primarily for evaluation. The choice is yours. Among these are the Lesson Quizzes, described here, and the Alternative Assessment, described under Summative Assessment, next. Because both of these assessments are provided for every lesson, you could use them both at different times.

Lesson Quizzes as Formative Assessment In this book, Lesson Quizzes in a unit follow the Unit Pretest. The five-item Lesson Quiz can be administered as a written test, used as an oral quiz, or given to small student groups for collaboration. In the Answer Key at the end of this book, you'll find a feature called the Test Doctor, which provides a brief explanation of what makes each correct answer correct and each incorrect answer incorrect. Use this explanatory material to begin a discussion following the quiz.

Classroom Observation

Classroom observation is one way to gather and record information that can lead to improved instruction. You'll find a Classroom Observation Checklist in Assessment Tools, following the Introduction.

Tips for Classroom Observation

- Don't try to see and record everything at once. Instead, identify specific skills you will observe in a session.

- Don't try to observe everyone at once. Focus on a few students at a time.

- Repeat observations at different times in order to identify patterns. This practice helps you validate or correct your impressions from a single time.

- Use the checklist as is or modify it to suit your students and your instruction. Fill in student names across the top and write the date next to the skills you are observing on a particular day.

- Keep the checklist, add to it, and consult it periodically for hints about strengths, weaknesses, and developments of particular students and of the class.

- Use your own system of ratings or the simple number code on the checklist. When you have not seen enough to give a rating, leave the space blank.

Summative Assessment

In the Student Edition

Visual Summary and Lesson Review

Interactive summaries help students synthesize lesson material, and the Lesson Review provides a variety of questions focusing on vocabulary, key concepts, and critical thinking.

Unit Reviews

Each unit in the Student Edition is followed by a Unit Review, also available in this Assessment Guide. These tests include the item types commonly found on the statewide assessments. You may want to use these tests to review unit content right away or at any time later in the year to help students prepare for the statewide assessment. If you wish to give students practice in filling in a machine-scorable answer sheet, use the bubble-type answer sheet at the start of the Answer Key.

In This Assessment Guide

Alternative Assessments

Every lesson has an Alternative Assessment worksheet, which is previewed in the Teacher Edition on the Evaluate page of the lesson. The activities on these worksheets assess student comprehension of core content, while at the same time offering a variety of options for students with various abilities, learning styles, and interests. The activities require students to produce a tangible product or to give a presentation that demonstrates their understanding of skills and concepts.

Tips for Alternative Assessment

- The structure of these worksheets allows for differentiation in topic, difficulty level, and activity type/learner preferences.

- Each worksheet has a variety of items for students and teachers to choose from.

- The items may relate to the entire lesson content or to just one or two key topics. Encourage students to select items so that they will hit most key topics in a lesson.

- Share the rubrics and Presentation Guidelines with students so they understand the expectations for these assignments. You could have them fill in a rubric with their name and activity choices at the same time they choose their assignments, and then submit the rubric with their presentation or assignment.

Grading Alternative Assessments

Each type of Alternative Assessment worksheet has a rubric for easy grading.

- The rubrics focus mostly on content comprehension, but also take into account presentation.

- The Answer Key describes the expected content mastery for each Alternative Assessment.

- Separate Presentation Guidelines describe the attributes of successful written work, posters and displays, oral presentations, and multimedia presentations.

- Each rubric has space to record your reasons for deducting points, such as content errors or particular presentation flaws.

- If you wish to change the focus of an Alternative Assessment worksheet, you can adjust the point values for the rubric.

The Presentation Guidelines and the rubrics follow the Introduction. The Answer Key appears at the end of the book.

Unit Tests A and B

This Assessment Guide contains leveled tests for each unit.

- The A-level tests are for students who typically perform below grade level.

- The B-level tests are intended for students whose performance is on grade level.

Both versions of the test address the unit content with a mixture of item types, including multiple choice, short response, and extended response. Both levels contains items of low, medium, and high cognitive complexity, though level B contains more items of higher complexity. A few items appear in both of the tests as a means of assuring parallel content coverage. If you need a higher-level test, you can easily assemble one from the lesson assessment banks in ExamView or online at thinkcentral.com. All items in the banks are tagged with five different measures of difficulty as well as standards and key terms.

End-of-Module Test

The final test in this Assessment Guide is the End-of-Module Review. This is a long-form, multiple-choice test in the style of the statewide assessments. An Answer Sheet appears with the review.

Performance-Based Assessment

Performance-Based Assessment involves a hands-on activity in which students demonstrate their skills and thought processes. Each Performance-Based Assessment includes a page of teacher-focused information and a general rubric for scoring. In addition to the Performance-Based Assessment provided for each unit, you can use many of the labs in the program as the basis for performance assessment.

Tips for Performance Assessment

- Prepare materials and stations so that all students have the same tasks. You may want to administer performance assessments to different groups over time.

- Provide clear expectations, including the measures on which students will be evaluated. You may invite them to help you formulate or modify the rubric.

- Assist students as needed, but avoid supplying answers to those who can handle the work on their own.

- Don't be hurried. Allow students enough time to do their best work.

Developing or Modifying a Rubric

Developing a rubric for a performance task involves three basic steps:

1. Identify the inquiry skills that are taught in the lesson and that students must perform to complete the task successfully and identify the understanding of content that is also required. Many of the skills may be found in the Lab and Activity Evaluation later in this guide.

2. Determine which skills and understandings of content are involved in each step.

3. Decide what you will look for to confirm that the student has acquired each skill and understanding you identified.

Portfolio Assessment, Guidelines

A portfolio is a showcase for student work, a place where many types of assignments, projects, reports and data sheets can be collected. The work samples in the collection provide snapshots of the student's efforts over time, and taken together they reveal the student's growth, attitudes, and understanding better than other types of assessment. Portfolio assessment involves meeting with each student to discuss the work and to set goals for future performance. In contrast with formal assessments, portfolio assessments have these advantages:

1. They give students a voice in the assessment process.

2. They foster reflection, self-monitoring, and self-evaluation.

3. They provide a comprehensive picture of a student's progress.

Tips for Portfolio Assessment

- Make a basic plan. Decide how many work samples will be included in the portfolios and what period of time they represent.

- Explain the portfolio and its use. Describe the portfolio an artist might put together, showing his or her best or most representative work, as part of an application for school or a job. The student's portfolio is based on this model.

- Together with your class decide on the required work samples that everyone's portfolio will contain.

- Explain that the students will choose additional samples of their work to include. Have students remember how their skills and understanding have grown over the period covered by the portfolio, and review their work with this in mind. The best pieces to choose may not be the longest or neatest.

- Give students the Portfolio Planning Worksheet found in Assessment Tools. Have students record their reasoning as they make their selections and assemble their portfolios.

- Share with students the Portfolio Evaluation Checklist, also found in Assessment Tools, and explain how you will evaluate the contents of their portfolios.

- Use the portfolios for conferences, grading, and planning. Give students the option of taking their portfolios home to share.

ASSESSMENT TOOLS
Alternative Assessment Presentation Guidelines

The following guidelines can be used as a starting point for evaluating student presentation of alternative assessments. For each category, use only the criteria that are relevant for the particular format you are evaluating; some criteria will not apply for certain formats.

Written Work
- Matches the assignment in format (essay, journal entry, newspaper report, etc.)
- Begins with a clear statement of the topic and purpose
- Provides information that is essential to the reader's understanding
- Supporting details are precise, related to the topic, and effective
- Follows a logical pattern of organization
- Uses transitions between ideas
- When appropriate, uses diagrams or other visuals
- Correct spelling, capitalization, and punctuation
- Correct grammar and usage
- Varied sentence structures
- Neat and legible

Posters and Displays
- Matches the assignment in format (brochure, poster, storyboard, etc.)
- Topic is well researched and quality information is presented
- Poster communicates an obvious, overall message
- Posters have large titles and the message, or purpose, is obvious
- Images are big, clear, and convey important information
- More important ideas and items are given more space and presented with larger images or text
- Colors are used for a purpose, such as to link words and images
- Sequence of presentation is easy to follow because of visual cues, such as arrows, letters, or numbers
- Artistic elements are appropriate and add to the overall presentation
- Text is neat
- Captions and labels have correct spelling, capitalization, and punctuation

Oral Presentations
- Matches the assignment in format (speech, news report, etc.)
- Presentation is delivered well, and enthusiasm is shown for topic
- Words are clearly pronounced and can easily be heard
- Information is presented in a logical, interesting sequence that the audience can follow
- Visual aids are relative to content, very neat, and artistic
- Often makes eye contact with audience
- Listens carefully to questions from the audience and responds accurately
- Stands straight, facing the audience
- Uses movements appropriate to the presentation; does not fidget
- Covers the topic well in the time allowed
- Gives enough information to clarify the topic, but does not include irrelevant details

Multimedia Presentations
- Topic is well researched, and essential information is presented
- The product shows evidence of an original and inventive approach
- The presentation conveys an obvious, overall message
- Contains all the required media elements, such as text, graphics, sounds, videos, and animations
- Fonts and formatting are used appropriately to emphasize words; color is used appropriately to enhance the fonts
- Sequence of presentation is logical and/or the navigation is easy and understandable
- Artistic elements are appropriate and add to the overall presentation
- The combination of multimedia elements with words and ideas produces an effective presentation
- Written elements have correct spelling, capitalization, and punctuation

Alternative Assessment Rubric – Tic-Tac-Toe

Worksheet Title: _____

Student Name: _____

Date: _____

Add the titles of each activity chosen to the chart below.

	Content (0-3 points)	**Presentation** (0-2 points)	*Points Sum*
Choice 1: _____			
Points			
Reason for missing points			
Choice 2: _____			
Points			
Reason for missing points			
Choice 3: _____			
Points			
Reason for missing points			
		Total Points (of 15 maximum)	

Alternative Assessment Rubric – Mix and Match

Worksheet Title: _____

Student Name: _____

Date: _____

Add the column choices to the chart below.

	Content (0-3 points)	**Presentation** (0-2 points)	*Points Sum*
Information Source from Column A: _____			
Topics Chosen for Column B: _____			
Presentation Format from Column C: _____			
Points			
Reason for missing points			
		Total Points (of 5 maximum)	

Alternative Assessment Rubric – Take Your Pick

Worksheet Title: _____

Student Name: _____

Date: _____

Add the titles of each activity chosen to the chart below.

	Content	**Presentation**	**Points Sum**
2-point item: 5-point item 8-point item:	*(0-1.5 points)* *(0-4 points)* *(0-6 points)*	*(0-0.5 point)* *(0-1 point)* *(0-2 points)*	
Choice 1: _____			
Points			
Reason for missing points			
Choice 2: _____			
Points			
Reason for missing points			
		Total Points (of 10 maximum)	

Alternative Assessment Rubric – Choose Your Meal

Worksheet Title: _____

Student Name: _____

Date: _____

Add the titles of each activity chosen to the chart below.

Appetizer, side dish, or dessert:	Content (0-3 points)	Presentation (0-2) points	Points Sum
Main Dish	(0-6 points)	(0-4 points)	
Appetizer: _____			
Points			
Reason for missing points			
Side Dish: _____			
Points			
Reason for missing points			
Main Dish: _____			
Points			
Reason for missing points			
Dessert: _____			
Points			
Reason for missing points			
		Total Points (of 25 maximum)	

Alternative Assessment Rubric – Points of View

Worksheet Title: _____

Student Name: _____

Date: _____

Add the titles of group's assignment to the chart below.

	Content *(0-4 points)*	**Presentation** *(0-1 points)*	*Points Sum*
Point of View:			
Points			
Reason for missing points			
		Total Points (of 5 maximum)	

Alternative Assessment Rubric – Climb the Pyramid

Worksheet Title: _____

Student Name: _____

Date: _____

Add the titles of each activity chosen to the chart below.

	Content *(0-3 points)*	**Presentation** *(0-2 points)*	*Points Sum*
Choice from bottom row: _____			
Points			
Reason for missing points			
Choice from middle row: _____			
Points			
Reason for missing points			
Top row: _____			
Points			
Reason for missing points			
		Total Points (of 15 maximum)	

Alternative Assessment Rubric – Climb the Ladder

Worksheet Title: _____

Student Name: _____

Date: _____

Add the titles of each activity chosen to the chart below.

	Content (0-3 points)	**Presentation** (0-2 points)	*Points Sum*
Choice 1 (top rung): _____			
Points			
Reason for missing points			
Choice 2 (middle rung): _____			
Points			
Reason for missing points			
Choice 3 (bottom rung): _____			
Points			
Reason for missing points			
		Total Points (of 15 maximum)	

Date _____

Rating Scale		
3 Outstanding	**1** Needs Improvement	
2 Satisfactory	☐ Not Enough Opportunity to Observe	

Names of Students

Inquiry Skills										
Observe										
Compare										
Classify/Order										
Gather, Record, Display, or Interpret Data										
Use Numbers										
Communicate										
Plan and Conduct Simple Investigations										
Measure										
Predict										
Infer										
Draw Conclusions										
Use Time/Space Relationships										
Hypothesize										
Formulate or Use Models										
Identify and Control Variables										
Experiment										

Lab and Activity Evaluation

Circle the appropriate number for each criterion. Then add up the circled numbers in each column and record the sum in the subtotals row at the bottom. Add up these subtotals to get the total score.

Graded by _____ Total _____ /100

Behavior	Completely	Mostly	Partially	Poorly
Follows lab procedures carefully and fully	10–9	8–7–6	5–4–3	2–1–0
Wears the required safety equipment and displays knowledge of safety procedures and hazards	10–9	8–7–6	5–4–3	2–1–0
Uses laboratory time productively and stays on task	10–9	8–7–6	5–4–3	2–1–0
Behavior	**Completely**	**Mostly**	**Partially**	**Poorly**
Uses tools, equipment, and materials properly	10–9	8–7–6	5–4–3	2–1–0
Makes quantitative observations carefully, with precision and accuracy	10–9	8–7–6	5–4–3	2–1–0
Uses the appropriate SI units to collect quantitative data	10–9	8–7–6	5–4–3	2–1–0
Records accurate qualitative data during the investigation	10–9	8–7–6	5–4–3	2–1–0
Records measurements and observations in clearly organized tables that have appropriate headings and units	10–9	8–7–6	5–4–3	2–1–0
Works well with partners	10–9	8–7–6	5–4–3	2–1–0
Efficiently and properly solves any minor problems that might occur with materials or procedures	10–9	8–7–6	5–4–3	2–1–0
Subtotals:				

Comments

_____

_____

_____

_____

Name _____ Date _____

My Science Portfolio

What Is in My Portfolio	Why I Chose It
1.	
2.	
3.	
4.	
5.	
6.	
7.	

I organized my Science Portfolio this way because _____

_____

_____

_____

_____

Portfolio Evaluation Checklist

Aspects of Science Literacy	Evidence of Growth
1. Understands science concepts *(Animals, Plants; Earth's Land, Air, Water; Space; Weather; Matter, Motion, Energy)*	_____ _____ _____
2. Uses inquiry skills *(observes, compares, classifies, gathers/ interprets data, communicates, measures, experiments, infers, predicts, draws conclusions)*	_____ _____ _____
3. Thinks critically *(analyzes, synthesizes, evaluates, applies ideas effectively, solves problems)*	_____ _____ _____
4. Displays traits/attitudes of a scientist *(is curious, questioning, persistent, precise, creative, enthusiastic; uses science materials carefully; is concerned for environment)*	_____ _____ _____

Summary of Portfolio Assessment

For This Review			Since Last Review		
Excellent	Good	Fair	Improving	About the Same	Not as Good

Introduction to Waves

Choose the letter of the best answer.

1. How can the speed of a mechanical wave be calculated?

   A. Add the wavelength and the period.

   B. Divide the period by the wavelength.

   C. Divide the wavelength by the period.

   D. Multiply the wavelength and the period.

2. A wave like the one shown in the diagram below is called a transverse wave. Such a wave is typical of light waves and other types of electromagnetic waves. Every transverse wave has certain properties, including wavelength. One measure of wavelength is the distance from B to D.

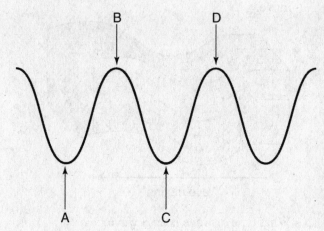

   What is another measure of wavelength?

   A. distance from A to D

   B. distance from A to C

   C. distance from B to C

   D. distance from A to B

3. What is one way that electromagnetic waves differ from mechanical waves?

   A. Electromagnetic waves move slower.

   B. Electromagnetic waves are longitudinal.

   C. Electromagnetic waves can travel through empty space.

   D. There is no difference between electromagnetic and mechanical waves.

4. Carrie is swimming in the ocean. As she floats over a large wave, her mother calls to her from the beach. What does the ocean wave have in common with the sound waves produced by Carrie's mother?

   A. Both kinds of waves progress through a medium.

   B. Both kinds of waves displace particles permanently.

   C. Neither kind of wave was caused by vibrations.

   D. Neither kind of wave transfers energy between particles.

5. What is the name of the lowest point of a wave?

   A. crest

   B. trough

   C. amplitude

   D. rest position

6. The diagram below shows a sound wave moving through air.

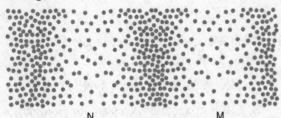

N   M

What about the diagram shows that the sound wave is a mechanical wave?

A. The sound wave causes vibration in air.

B. The sound wave was made by a machine.

C. The sound wave causes extra air particles to form.

D. The sound wave vibrates perpendicular to the direction of the wave motion.

7. A wave is produced from a vibrating string on a violin. Two observers are standing 20 m and 40 m away from the musician. The observer that is further away states that the violin sounds quiet but the other observer disagrees. What best explains the different experiences of the two observers?

A. The energy of the sound wave increased as it moved away from the source.

B. The energy of the sound wave decreased as it moved away from the source.

C. The energy of the sound wave remained the same as it moved away from the source.

D. The energy of the sound wave increased, then decreased as it moved away from the source.

8. Which of these is a mechanical wave?

A. light

B. sound

C. gamma ray

D. electromagnetic

9. Through which of these media do sound waves travel most slowly?

A. iron

B. wood

C. water

D. cold air

10. Tony is studying the types of waves that occur during earthquakes. He finds a diagram of an S wave that shows how the wave makes the Earth move.

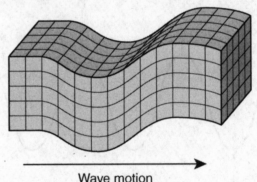

Wave motion

What type of wave is an S wave?

A. sound

B. transverse

C. longitudinal

D. electromagnetic

Waves

Choose the letter of the best answer.

1. Astronomers study radio waves to learn about the universe. Why might radio waves be used to study objects in space?

   A. They are sound waves that cause vibrations in stars and planets.

   B. They are electromagnetic waves, so they don't require a medium.

   C. They are mechanical waves that pass through interstellar particles.

   D. They are longitudinal waves, which create compressions in the fabric of space.

2. A student makes a transverse wave by shaking a rope tied to a doorknob up and down. Which statement accurately describes the wave in the rope?

   A. Each part of the rope moves in the same direction as the wave.

   B. Each part of the rope moves up and down as the wave moves toward the door.

   C. Each part of the rope moves up and down as the wave moves around in circles.

   D. Each part of the rope moves up and down as the entire wave moves up and down.

3. Which is the best description of a wave?

   A. energy that makes particles move

   B. a disturbance that transfers energy

   C. a disruption causing the transfer of matter

   D. any type of matter that vibrates back and forth

4. A wave produced by an earthquake appears in the diagram below:

   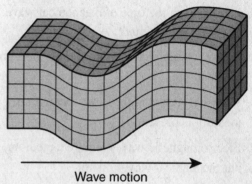

   Wave motion

   A second wave leaves the center of an earthquake at the same time. The second wave is a longitudinal wave. After 10 seconds, will the two waves travel the same distance?

   A. Yes, because both waves are longitudinal waves.

   B. Yes, because all waves travel at the same speed in similar mediums.

   C. No, because only one type of wave can travel through a medium at a time.

   D. No, because transverse waves travel at different speeds than longitudinal waves.

5. A whale makes a noise underwater that is too low-pitched for humans to hear. What type of wave is this?

   A. S wave

   B. visible light

   C. mechanical

   D. electromagnetic

Properties of Waves

Choose the letter of the best answer.

1. The speed of a mechanical wave through a medium depends on the type of medium. It also depends on the type of mechanical wave. Which statement is true?

   A. All waves travel at the same speed through any medium.

   B. All waves travel at the same speed if no medium is present.

   C. Electromagnetic waves require a medium, but mechanical waves do not.

   D. Mechanical waves require a medium, but electromagnetic waves do not.

2. The diagram below shows a wave pattern. One wave property that is shown is amplitude. Amplitude is the vertical distance from the rest position to either the crest or the trough of a wave.

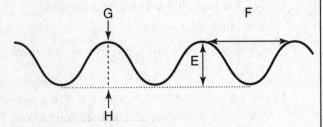

   What is the rest position of a wave in the diagram?

   A. E

   B. F

   C. distance from G to H

   D. point that is halfway between G and H

3. Brianna reported a measurement in units of hertz. What property of a wave was she measuring?

   A. period

   B. frequency

   C. amplitude

   D. wavelength

4. During a thunderstorm, Sanjay saw lightning and then heard thunder 5 seconds later. What would be different if the air had been warmer?

   A. He would have seen the lightning and heard the thunder at the same time.

   B. He would have heard the thunder before seeing the lightning.

   C. He would have heard the thunder sooner.

   D. He would have heard the thunder later.

5. Aimee and Patrick are playing hide-and-seek on a summer day. Aimee gives Patrick a clue to her location by knocking three times every 30 seconds. Which characteristic of waves makes this a useful clue to help Patrick find Aimee?

   A. Wave energy increases with distance.

   B. Wave energy decreases with distance.

   C. Sound waves travel faster in cold air than in warm air.

   D. Sound waves travel faster in warm air than in cold air.

Waves

Take Your Pick: *What Are Waves?*
Complete the activities to show what you've learned about waves.

1. Work on your own, with a partner, or with a small group.

2. Choose items below for a total of 10 points. Check your choices.

3. Have your teacher approve your plan.

4. Submit or present your results.

2 Points

_____ **Everyday Waves** Design a poster about a situation in which a wave is involved. Indicate and label the wave featured on your poster, and explain whether the wave is mechanical or electromagnetic.

_____ **Making Waves** Create models that show both transverse and longitudinal waves. Label each type of wave.

5 Points

_____ **You Ask the Questions** Write five questions about mechanical waves. On the back of your paper, write the answers to your questions.

_____ **Helping a Friend** Suppose your friend is just about to begin studying waves in his or her science class. Your friend asks you to help explain what a wave is and how a wave is different from its medium. Write a dialogue between you and your friend in which you answer your friend's questions.

_____ **The Wave Game** Play a game in which you identify electromagnetic and mechanical waves. Write the following types of waves on index cards: ocean waves, earthquake waves, sound waves, visible light, ultraviolet light, X-rays, radio waves, and microwaves. Create two columns on the board or on paper and label them "Electromagnetic" and "Mechanical." Shuffle the cards and try to put each type of wave in the correct category.

_____ **Paragraph Paraphrase** Paraphrase what you have learned about electromagnetic waves. Be sure to include the most important pieces of information.

8 Points

_____ **Which Wave Are You?** Write and perform a skit in which one actor is a transverse wave and the other actor is a longitudinal wave. Have the actors also act out the way their waves move. Then actors should talk about the similarities and differences between the way they move.

_____ **Compare and Contrast Waves** Make a presentation in which you compare and contrast mechanical waves and electromagnetic waves. Discuss the ways the two types of waves are the same and the ways they are different. Give examples of each type of wave.

Properties of Waves

Choose Your Meal: *Describing Wave Properties*
Show what you have learned about different types of waves and their properties.

1. Work on your own, with a partner, or with a small group.

2. Choose one item from each section of the menu, with an optional dessert. Check your choices.

3. Have your teacher approve your plan.

4. Submit or present your results.

Appetizers

_____ **Make a Graph** Make a graph of a transverse wave that has an amplitude of 2 cm and a wavelength of 10 cm. Show at least two full wave cycles on your graph. Include necessary labels.

_____ **Make a Model** Make a model of a transverse wave that has an amplitude of 10 cm and a wavelength of 25 cm. Show at least two full wave cycles.

_____ **Make a Diagram** Make a diagram of a transverse wave that has an amplitude of 20 cm and a wavelength of 30 cm. Show at least two full wave cycles.

Main Dish

_____ **Calculate Speed** Choose the amplitude and wavelength figures of one of the transverse waves above, and calculate the wave speeds, given the following periods: 0.5 s, 2.25 s, 10 s, and 35 s.

Side Dishes

_____ **Design a Poster** Develop a poster that explains what wave speed is and what factors play a role in determining wave speed. Be sure to include information for both mechanical and electromagnetic waves.

_____ **Concept Map** Make a concept map that explains how amplitude, wavelength, and frequency are related to the energy of a wave.

Desserts (optional)

_____ **Investigate Music** Find out how frequency and wavelength are related to musical notes. Develop a demonstration to show the relationship and perform it for your class.

_____ **Comparing Waves** Draw a transverse wave and a longitudinal wave. Choose a method and show how they are similar and how they are different.

Comparing Sound Waves and Light Waves

Purpose In this activity, students observe different effects of light waves and sound waves, and use their observations to compare the two kinds of waves.

Time Period 30 minutes

Preparation Provide each pair with the materials they need to complete the activity. Have paper towels on hand in case of water spills.

Safety Tips Wipe up any spills immediately. Make sure students observe safe procedures for handling electricity.

Teaching Strategies This activity works best in pairs. You may want to explain that a tuning fork is designed to produce a sound wave with a specific frequency. In music, these frequencies correspond to specific musical notes. Demonstrate how to hit the tuning fork on the sole of a shoe. Alternatively, you can have students strike the tuning fork on a rubber mallet or rubber stopper.

Scoring Rubric

Possible points	Performance indicators
0–20	Appropriate use of materials and equipment
0–30	Quality and clarity of observations
0–50	Explanation of observations

Name _____ Date _____

Comparing Sound Waves and Light Waves

Objective

You have learned about mechanical waves and electromagnetic waves. Mechanical waves travel through a medium, like air or water. Electromagnetic waves can travel without a medium. In this activity, you will observe the effects of both light waves and sound waves, and use your observations to classify and compare these two kinds of waves.

Know the Score!

As you work through this activity, keep in mind that you will be earning a grade for the following:

- how well you work with the materials and equipment (20%)
- the quality and clarity of your observations (30%)
- how well you use your observations to answer analysis questions (50%)

Materials and Equipment

- bowl, metal or plastic
- flashlight
- paper towels

- tuning fork, any frequency
- water

Safety Information

- Clean up any spills immediately.
- Be sure to keep electrical devices away from water.

Procedure

1. Fill ¾ of the bowl with water.

2. Shine the flashlight into the water without letting the flashlight touch the water. Observe the surface of the water. Record your observations.

_____

_____

_____

3. Turn off the flashlight and set it aside.

4. Strike the tuning fork against the sole of a shoe and hold it above the surface of the water. Do not let the tuning fork actually touch the water. Observe the surface of the water. Record your observations.

_____

_____

_____

Analysis

5. Compare the effect of light waves and sound waves on the water that you observed.

_____

_____

6. Classify light waves and sound waves as mechanical or electromagnetic.

_____

_____

7. Based on what you know about mechanical and electromagnetic waves, explain what you observed in Steps 2 and 4.

_____

_____

_____

_____

Unit 1: Introduction to Waves

Vocabulary
Fill in each blank with the term that best completes the following sentences.

1. Light travels as a(n) _____ wave.

2. The distance from the crest of one wave to the crest of the next wave is the _____ .

3. _____, the number of waves produced in a given amount of time, is expressed in Hertz.

4. Sound is a(n) _____ wave because it cannot travel without a medium.

5. The maximum distance that the particles of a medium move away from their rest position is a measure of a wave's _____.

Key Concepts
Read each question below, and circle the best answer.

6. Sashita uses the volume control on her TV to make the sound louder or softer. Which property of waves is Sashita's volume control changing?

   A. amplitude

   B. wave period

   C. wavelength

   D. wave speed

7. Which statement best explains what waves are?

   A. wavy lines on graph paper

   B. disturbances that transfer energy

   C. light energy that changes into particles of matter

   D. circles that move out from a central place

8. The diagram shows the shape and different measurements of a wave.

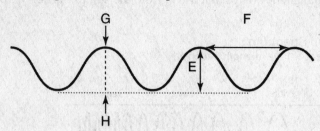

What property of the wave does F measure?

A. period   C. amplitude

B. frequency   D. wavelength

9. Which type of electromagnetic wave has the highest frequency?

A. radio waves   C. light waves

B. gamma rays   D. x-rays

10. Isabella researched how waves travel through the ground during an earthquake. She drew a diagram of one, called an S wave, moving through Earth's crust.

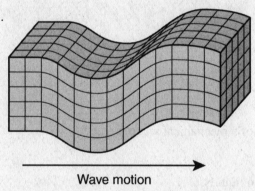

Wave motion

Based on her diagram, what kind of wave is an S wave?

A. light

B. sound

C. longitudinal

D. transverse

11. Visible, infrared, and ultraviolet light are electromagnetic waves that travel from the sun to Earth. There are other types of electromagnetic waves as well.

The Electromagnetic Spectrum
Typical frequency in hertz (1 hertz = 1 wavelength/second)

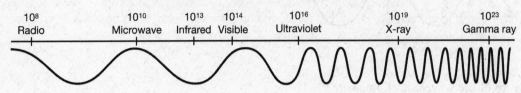

10^8	10^{10}	10^{13}	10^{14}	10^{16}	10^{19}	10^{23}
Radio	Microwave	Infrared	Visible	Ultraviolet	X-ray	Gamma ray

Which statement best explains what electromagnetic waves are?

A. waves that vibrate through a medium

B. disturbances in the atmosphere of space

C. disturbances in electric and magnetic fields

D. slow-moving waves

12. Frequency equals the number of wavelengths per unit of time.

$$\text{Frequency} = \frac{\text{Wavelengths}}{\text{Unit of time}}$$

Which unit is used to measure frequency as cycles per second?

A. hertz   C. crest

B. period   D. minutes

13. Which statement about the effects of medium on the speed of a mechanical wave is true?

A. Medium has no effect on the speed of a mechanical wave.

B. A mechanical wave generally travels faster in solids than liquids.

C. A mechanical wave generally travels faster in gases than liquids.

D. A mechanical wave always travels through liquids at the speed of light.

Critical Thinking
Answer the following questions in the space provided.

14. Some waves carry more energy than others. Which wave has more energy, a loud sound or a quiet sound? Why?

_____

_____

15. Tafari worked one summer on a ship that set weather buoys in the ocean. He watched how one of the buoys moved in the water.

Which wave property describes why the buoy bobs up and down?

Which wave property determined how fast the buoys bobbed in the water?

He observed that when the wind blew harder, the ocean waves were larger, and the buoys moved away from the ship. What effect, if any, did the waves have on how far the buoys moved? Explain your answer.

_____

_____

_____

_____

Connect ESSENTIAL QUESTIONS

Lessons 1 and 2

Answer the following question in the space provided.

16. Jung arrived at a concert in the park so late that the only seat she could get was almost a block from the stage. The music sounded much fainter to Jung than it did to people near the stage. She could hear the drums and bass guitar fairly well, but she had trouble hearing higher sounds from the singer. Explain the properties and behavior of waves that affected how Jung heard the music.

_____

_____

_____

_____

_____

_____

Introduction to Waves

Key Concepts
Choose the letter of the best answer.

1. Suppose a mechanical wave is traveling through medium A. When the wave enters medium B, it speeds up. Which of the following statements can be **true** about medium A and medium B?

   A. Medium A is a solid and medium B is a gas.

   B. Medium A is a liquid and medium B is a solid.

   C. Medium A is a gas and medium B is a vacuum.

   D. Medium A is a vacuum and medium B is a liquid.

2. What is the term for the distance from the highest part of one wave to the highest part of the next wave?

   A. period

   B. frequency

   C. amplitude

   D. wavelength

3. Caleb is at the beach. He counts the number of wave peaks that pass a given point on the beach in a certain amount of time. What property of waves does Caleb measure?

   A. speed

   B. frequency

   C. amplitude

   D. wavelength

4. Carlos is studying electromagnetic waves. He finds a diagram of the electromagnetic spectrum shown below, but it is missing a label.

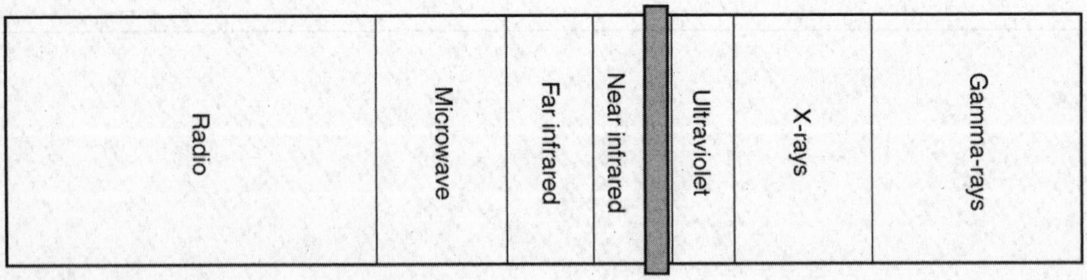

   What is the proper label of the unlabeled region?

   A. radar

   B. television

   C. visible light

   D. cosmic rays

5. An earthquake sends out mechanical waves in all directions from its source. In answering the following question, assume the wave starts carrying energy equally in all directions. The wavefront reaches each of the different locations as shown in the diagram.

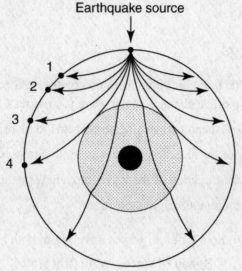

At which location does a point on the wavefront have the **least** energy?

A. 1

B. 2

C. 3

D. 4

6. In which direction do longitudinal waves travel?

A. They travel in random directions.

B. They travel around in a circular motion.

C. They travel parallel to the direction of the disturbance.

D. They travel perpendicular to the direction of the disturbance.

7. Through which medium does a mechanical wave travel most quickly?

A. solid

B. liquid

C. less dense gas

D. very dense gas

8. What is the speed of a wave with a wavelength of 4 cm and a frequency of 8 hertz?

    A. 0.5 cm/s

    B. 2 cm/s

    C. 12 cm/s

    D. 32 cm/s

9. A wave passes through a medium. The particles in the medium change their position. Which statement best describes how the position of a particle changes as the wave progresses?

    A. The particle moves in one direction, then the opposite, and returns to its original position.

    B. The particle moves perpendicular to the direction of the wave into a new position

    C. The particle moves parallel with the direction of the wave into a new position.

    D. The particle vibrates continually around its original position.

10. The graph below shows the speeds of three different waves traveling in both air and water.

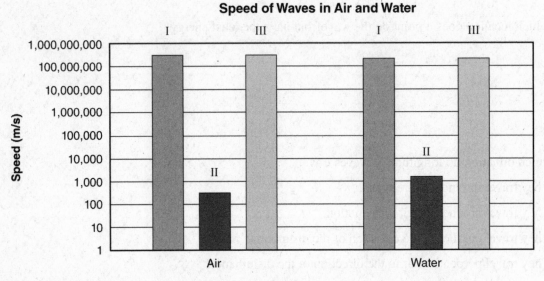

Speed of Waves in Air and Water

What evidence suggests that wave II is a mechanical wave?

A. Mechanical waves cannot pass through solids, which is why the data are missing.

B. Mechanical waves do not travel faster than 5,000 m/s.

C. Wave II lacks the amplitudes of wave I.

D. Its speed differs depending on the medium.

11. All mechanical waves have which of the following in common?

    A. Mechanical waves are transverse.

    B. Mechanical waves are longitudinal.

    C. Mechanical waves do not require a medium to move.

    D. Mechanical waves must progress through a medium.

12. A loud motorcycle passes by the front of Bill's house. What medium does the sound wave travel through to get from the motorcycle to Bill's ears?

    A. air

    B. energy

    C. a vacuum

    D. large vibrations

Name _____ Date _____

Critical Thinking

Answer the following questions in the space provided.

13. Compare the sound waves created by a tuning fork in water and in air.

_____

_____

_____

Extended Response

Answer the following questions in the space provided.

14. An alarm clock is placed in a sealed container without any air. Describe what you will observe when the alarm clock goes off. Justify your reasoning.

_____

_____

_____

_____

_____

Introduction to Waves

Key Concepts
Choose the letter of the best answer.

1. A mechanical waves passes through two media, medium A and medium B. If the wave's speed decreases when passing from medium A into medium B, which of the following is true?

   A. Medium A is a solid and medium B is a gas.

   B. Medium A is a liquid and medium B is a solid.

   C. Medium A is a solid and medium B is a vacuum.

   D. Medium A is a vacuum and medium B is a liquid.

2. Which term describes the length between two adjacent crests of a wave?

   A. period

   B. frequency

   C. amplitude

   D. wavelength

3. Brenda is listening for a beacon when she hears a continuous series of beeps. The time between the beeps is 2 seconds. What is the best way for her to enter her observations in her log book?

   A. The amplitude of the beacon is 2.

   B. The speed of the beacon is 2 m/s.

   C. The frequency of the beacon is 0.5 Hz.

   D. The wavelength of the beacon is 0.5 nm.

4. Julia is studying electromagnetic waves. She finds a diagram of the electromagnetic spectrum shown below, but it is missing a label.

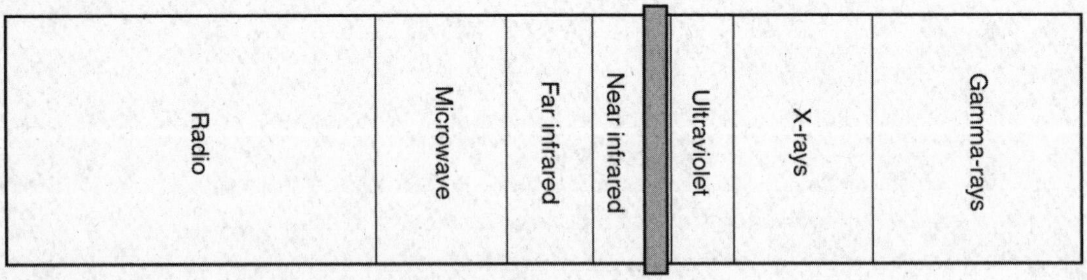

Radio		Microwave	Far infrared	Near infrared		Ultraviolet	X-rays		Gamma-rays

   What must be true of the waves represented by the missing label?

   A. They are vibrating in electric and magnetic fields.

   B. They cause particles to vibrate parallel to the wave motion.

   C. They travel faster in a vacuum than the waves to their left in the diagram.

   D. They travel faster in a vacuum than the waves to their right in the diagram.

5. A devastating earthquake occurs in a heavily populated area, releasing waves in all directions from its source. In answering the following question, assume the wave starts carrying energy equally in all directions. The wavefront reaches each of the different locations shown in the diagram.

Earthquake source

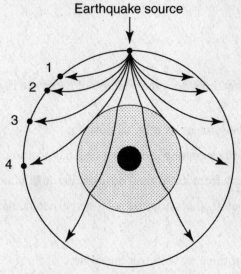

The mayor wants to send medical personnel to the area that likely experienced the most damage. Which location should the mayor send the personnel **first**?

A. 1

B. 2

C. 3

D. 4

6. A driver of a car honks the car horn at a dog in the street. The horn produces longitudinal waves. The dog hears the horn and runs out of the street before the car gets close. Which statement correctly describes why the dog was able to hear the car horn?

A. Longitudinal waves travel in random directions.

B. Longitudinal waves travel around in a circular motion.

C. Longitudinal waves travel parallel to the direction of the disturbance.

D. Longitudinal waves travel perpendicular to the direction of the disturbance.

7. Wave speed depends on the properties of the medium through which a wave travels. In which medium will a mechanical wave travel fastest?

A. hot air

B. cold air

C. a liquid

D. a solid

8. What is the speed of a wave with a wavelength ( ) cm and a frequency of 4 hertz?

   A. 0.4 cm/s

   B. 2.5 cm/s

   C. 14 cm/s

   D. 40 cm/s

9. After a wave passes through a medium, how does the position of a particle in that medium compare to its original position?

   A. The particle's position is about the same as its original position.

   B. The particle's position is continually vibrating around its original position.

   C. The particle's position moves away from its original position in the direction of the wave.

   D. The particle's position moves away from its original position perpendicular to the direction of the wave.

10. The graph below shows the speeds of three waves in air and water.

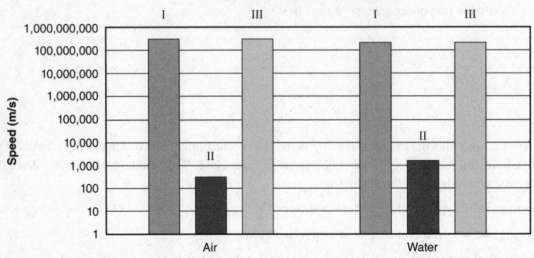

Speed of Waves in Air and Water

Which wave(s) are electromagnetic waves?

   A. II only

   B. I, II, and III

   C. I and II only

   D. I and III only

11. Which of these statements describes a characteristic of all mechanical waves?

   A. They travel through media.

   B. They are transverse waves.

   C. They are longitudinal waves.

   D. They travel through empty space.

12. Alex hears a loud rumble as he watches a space shuttle lift off from the launch pad. What medium does the sound wave travel through to get from the shuttle to Alex's ears?

   A. air

   B. energy

   C. a vacuum

   D. large vibrations

Critical Thinking
Answer the following questions in the space provided.

13. Andrew and his partner are divers. They are working underwater, 10 m apart, on an oil platform. Josh and his partner are working, also 10 m apart, on the part of the platform that is above water. Andrew and Josh each make a loud noise of the same volume at the same time. Whose partner hears the noise first? Explain your answer.

_____

_____

Extended Response

Answer the following questions in the space provided.

14. Compare the vibrations involved in creating mechanical waves and electromagnetic waves. Use a ripple in a pond and a light wave traveling though water as examples.

_____

_____

_____

_____

_____

Sound

Choose the letter of the best answer.

1. The medium through which a sound wave passes can be a solid, a liquid, or a gas. Properties of a wave might change when it moves from one medium to another. What happens to the speed of a sound wave when the medium changes from a gas to a solid?

   A. It speeds up.

   B. It slows down.

   C. It remains the same.

   D. It speeds up and then slows down.

2. A particular digital encoding technology consists of a sequence of pits on its surface, as shown below.

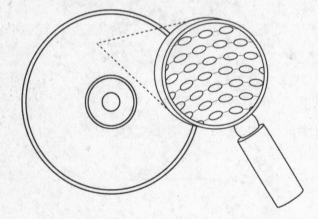

   How do the pits enable sounds to be produced?

   A. The pits store the actual sound waves.

   B. The pits store data used to create sound.

   C. The pits are created by the sound waves.

   D. The pits are not related to the production of sound.

3. An ambulance has its siren on. What direction is the ambulance moving relative to you if the siren is decreasing in pitch?

   A. behind you

   B. toward you

   C. away from you

   D. maintaining the same position

4. The image below shows a sound wave from a radio transmitter. What will be the effect on points B and D if the frequency decreases?

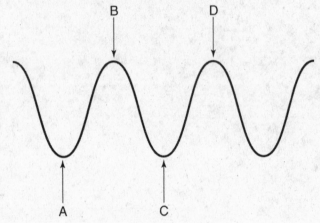

   A. B and D will increase in height.

   B. B and D will decrease in height.

   C. The distance between B and D will increase.

   D. The distance between B and D will decrease.

5. What type of waves does the human ear convert to electric signals during the process of hearing?

   A. electromagnetic waves

   B. longitudinal waves

   C. transverse waves

   D. ultrasonic waves

6. In which of the following settings would sound waves travel the fastest through the air?

   A. a cool, rainy day in Seattle

   B. a desert in southern Texas

   C. a winter day in North Dakota

   D. in orbit around Earth

7. Which kind of waves involve the compression of particles?

   A. light waves

   B. water waves

   C. transverse waves

   D. longitudinal waves

8. A sound is produced near a large wall. What process causes the wave to bounce back, as shown in the image?

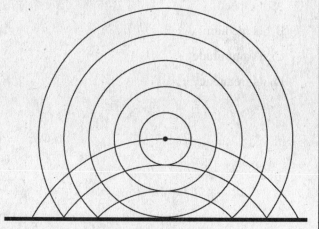

   A. constructive interference

   B. destructive interference

   C. absorption

   D. reflection

9. A sonic boom is produced by a jet. What can you determine about the jet's motion?

   A. It is increasing in altitude.

   B. Its engines produced a backfire.

   C. It is traveling faster than the speed of sound.

   D. It is near a mountain where echoes can be produced.

10. What happens during an ultrasound procedure to produce an image of a patient's body?

   A. Ultrasonic waves reflect off the patient's internal organs.

   B. Ultraviolet waves reflect off the patient's internal organs.

   C. Ultrasonic waves pass through the patient's internal organs.

   D. Ultraviolet waves pass through the patient's internal organs.

Sound Waves and Hearing

Choose the letter of the best answer.

1. The diagram below shows a sound wave moving through air.

    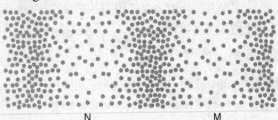

    What property of the wave would change if the distance between points N and M was longer?

    A. The pitch would decrease.

    B. The loudness would decrease.

    C. The amplitude would increase.

    D. The frequency would increase.

2. A large explosion can damage a person's hearing. What causes this damage?

    A. Heat from the explosion burns the eardrum.

    B. The explosion triggers smaller explosions inside the ear.

    C. Transverse waves from the explosion cause vibrations that damage the ear.

    D. Compression waves from the explosion cause vibrations that damage the ear.

3. When sound waves move through a medium, in what direction do the particles in the medium move?

    A. The particles always move side to side.

    B. The particles always move up and down.

    C. The particles always move in the same direction as the wave.

    D. The particles always move perpendicular to the direction of the wave.

4. What role does the inner ear play in hearing sounds?

    A. It blocks out unwanted sounds.

    B. It converts vibrations into electrical signals.

    C. It helps determine if a sound is in front of or behind you.

    D. It reflects high and low frequencies back to their source.

5. What property of a wave changes to create the Doppler effect?

    A. its speed

    B. its medium

    C. its amplitude

    D. its frequency

Interactions of Sound Waves

Choose the letter of the best answer.

1. A car with loud bass speakers drives by a house. The windows of the house vibrate significantly. What term best describes why the windows vibrate?

   A. interference

   B. resonance

   C. reflection

   D. echoing

2. The following bar graph shows the speeds of a wave in air and water.

   Speed of Waves in Air and in Water

   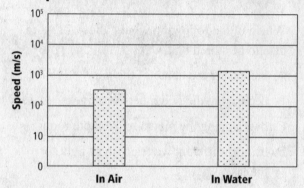

   How would the wave speeds change if the temperature of the air and water were both increased equally?

   A. Neither would increase in speed.

   B. Both waves would increase in speed.

   C. The wave in air would increase in speed.

   D. The wave in water would increase in speed.

3. What is the best explanation for why, on average, children playing inside a house are louder than those playing outside?

   A. Sound waves can reflect off many walls and surfaces.

   B. Houses are heated, so sound waves travel faster in the air.

   C. Constructive interference from walls and wood floors is common.

   D. Vibrations in the windows causes the sounds to intensify.

4. A hiker is in the Grand Canyon. Which surface would provide the clearest echo?

   A. the rocky canyon walls

   B. the thick desert shrubs

   C. the sandy riverbank

   D. the surface of the river

5. Two friends are at a concert. They discover a location in the auditorium where the band sounds significantly louder than in other places. What is the best explanation for the strengthening of the sound?

   A. constructive interference

   B. destructive interference

   C. medium temperature

   D. resonance

Sound Technology

Choose the letter of the best answer.

1. Which of the following is a type of echolocation used to create images of objects that could otherwise not be seen inside the human body?

   A. sonar technology

   B. radar technology

   C. frequency technology

   D. ultrasound technology

2. Echolocation refers to the reflection of what kind of waves?

   A. light waves

   B. sound waves

   C. ultraviolet waves only

   D. ultrasonic waves only

3. Which parts of a telephone involve the conversion of sound waves to electrical signals?

   A. the speaker

   B. the microphone

   C. both the speaker and the microphone

   D. neither the speaker nor the microphone

4. How can sonar be used?

   A. It can be used to locate underwater objects.

   B. It can be used in microscopic surgery.

   C. It can be used to locate objects in outer space.

   D. It can be used in creating images of internal organs.

5. The following diagram shows a close-up of the surface of a CD.

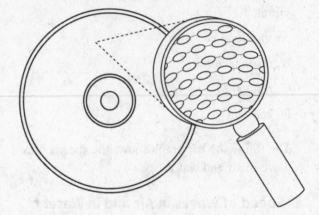

   Which of the following would allow for more data to be stored on a CD?

   A. increasing the depth of the pits

   B. decreasing the width between tracks

   C. overlapping the pits to make more room

   D. using a different wavelength of light for the laser

Sound Waves and Hearing

Climb the Ladder: *Sound Studies*

Select an idea from each rung of the ladder to show what you've learned about the different ways to represent data.

1. Work on your own, with a partner, or with a small group.

2. Choose one item from each rung of the ladder. Check your choices.

3. Have your teacher approve your plan.

4. Submit or present your results.

__ Make a Two- or Three-Dimensional Model Make a model that illustrates an important topic from this lesson, such as the human ear, a sound wave, or the Doppler effect. Include labels and an explanation of the concepts you are depicting.	**__ Make a Digital Presentation** Prepare a digital presentation about the characteristics of sound waves. Present your findings to the class using your poster and audio recordings of animal calls.
__ Gather Data and Make a Bar Graph Go online and research the decibel levels of 10 common sounds. Use this information to create a bar graph that can be used to compare the noise levels of the sounds.	**__ Write a Story** Write a story from the perspective of a sound wave. The story should start with the sound wave being produced and should continue until it reaches the cochlea in the inner ear. Describe the sound wave in terms of loudness and pitch along with the parts of the outer, middle, and inner ear.
__ Make a Crossword Puzzle Using the vocabulary terms from this lesson and at least five other terms found in this lesson, create a crossword puzzle. The clues for the terms can be definitions, descriptions, or examples. Include a solution key.	**__ Write and Perform a Skit** Write a skit in which the characters discuss the risks of loud noises and ways to avoid hearing damage. Make sure that your skit includes an explanation of why hearing damage can occur and describes which types of sounds can be damaging.

Interactions of Sound Waves

Tic-Tac-Toe: *Design a Concert Hall*

You are on a committee that is designing a concert hall. Think about the best design that addresses the issues below.

1. Work on your own, with a partner, or with a small group.

2. Choose three activities. Check the boxes you plan to complete. They must form a straight line in any direction.

3. Have your teacher approve your plan.

4. Do each activity, and turn in your results.

__ I Can't Hear You!	__ Echo, Echo, Echo	__ Stay Out!
Give an oral explanation about how someone in one seat in the audience might hear loud sounds (constructive interference), but another person might hear quiet sounds (destructive interference).	Draw a sketch that shows the stage and the concert hall walls. Use arrows to show where the sound will go. Draw the stage so that a performer in center stage will not hear any echoes of her music.	Write a plan that explains how you will keep the outside street noise out of the concert hall. Explain what materials you will use to absorb or reflect sounds as needed.
__ What a Pit!	__ Too Much Noise!	__ Constructive Criticism
Draw a sketch showing an orchestra pit. Show how the sounds of the instruments work together to create constructive interference.	Neighbors are worried about noise. Prepare a PowerPoint or poster presentation that tells them the features that you can incorporate into your design to absorb noise, so that the neighbors can sleep during nighttime performances.	Make a model that shows how you can use constructive interference to make the concert enjoyable to the most members of the audience. Show where the musicians should be placed in relation to audience members.
__ A Resounding Success	__ Tuning Up	__ Standing Wave
Give a demonstration to the committee that explains what is happening to someone in the audience who feels resonance in their body while listening to the music. What can be done to increase or decrease these vibrations?	Write instructions explaining how to use a tuning fork to tune the piano in the concert hall.	Make a diagram that shows the standing wave made by a wind instrument when it is played. Where does the air go? Why do the sounds get louder when they form a standing wave?

Sound Technology

Climb the Pyramid: *Sound by Sound*

1. Work on your own, with a partner, or with a small group.

2. Choose one item from each layer of the pyramid. Check your choices.

3. Have your teacher approve your plan.

4. Submit or present your results.

__ **Sound Technology in Everyday Life**

Identify three examples of sound technology innovations that have changed your life. Research the innovations you have chosen and describe briefly how each works.

__ **Sonar**

Research how sonar can make undersea exploration easier and more effective. Include information about a situation in which scientists used sonar to map the floor of the sea or shipwrecks.

__ **Historical Speeches**

Listen to a well-known speech from history that was recorded and saved. Explain what the recording of that speech means to our lives today. Share the recording with your classmates.

__ **MP3 Players**

Find out how digital sound files store a large amount of information. Research an MP3 player or other devices that store sound files. Give a short oral report summarizing what you have learned.

__ **Echolocation**

Identify three animals that use echolocation. Research to find out how they locate objects and what kinds of objects they seek. Prepare a poster to share what you learn.

__ **Ultrasound in Medicine**

Interview a medical professional or do other research to learn about the use of ultrasound in medicine. Write a short report that explains how ultrasound can be used. Include ultrasound pictures if available.

Frequency and Pitch

Purpose In this activity, students will use tuning forks to demonstrate the relationship between pitch and frequency.

Time Period 30 minutes

Preparation It will be easiest for students to observe the difference in pitch between two tuning forks if the forks are obviously different in size. If possible, give each group a large fork and a small one.

Teaching Strategies This activity works best in groups of 2 or 3 students, although you may be limited by the number of tuning forks available. You may want to explain that each tuning fork is designed to produce a sound wave with a certain frequency. In music, these frequencies correspond to specific musical notes. Demonstrate how to hit the tuning fork on the sole of a shoe, a rubber mallet, or rubber stopper.

Scoring Rubric

Possible points	Performance indicators
0–10	Appropriate use of materials and equipment
0–50	Making and recording observations
0–40	Analysis of observations

Frequency and Pitch

Objective

You have learned that sound waves have specific properties, including wavelength and frequency. In this activity, you will use what you know about sound waves to demonstrate the relationship between frequency of a sound wave and its pitch.

Know the Score!

As you work through this activity, keep in mind that you will be earning a grade for the following:

- how well you work with the materials and equipment (10%)

- the quality and clarity of your observations (50%)

- how well you analyze your observations (40%)

Materials and Equipment

- solid object, such as a table or desk

- tuning forks with different frequencies (2)

Procedure

1. Observe the two tuning forks without touching them. Write your observations below.

    _____

    _____

2. Which tuning fork do you predict will have a higher pitch?

    _____

3. Pick up the larger tuning fork and strike it firmly against the sole of your shoe. Hold it in the air without letting it touch anything. Let it continue until you can't hear the sound it makes anymore.

4. Now, strike the same tuning fork against your shoe a second time. Instead of holding it in the air, touch the base of the handle to a solid object such as a desk or table.

5. What difference did you observe between holding the tuning fork in the air and touching it to the solid object? Record your observations.

    _____

    _____

6. Repeat steps 3–5 using the smaller tuning fork. Record your observations.

    _____

    _____

Analysis

7. How are the physical sizes of the tuning forks related to their frequencies?

   _____

   _____

8. Which tuning fork had the higher pitch? Was the prediction you made in Step 2 correct?

   _____

   _____

9. How is pitch related to frequency?

   _____

   _____

10. Explain what you observed in Steps 5 and 6.

   _____

   _____

Unit 2: Sound

Vocabulary

Check the box to show whether each statement is true or false.

T	F	
☐	☐	1. A Sound wave is a <u>longitudinal wave</u> that is caused by vibrations in a medium.
☐	☐	2. <u>Decibels</u> are units that measure the pitch of a sound.
☐	☐	3. An <u>echo</u> is a sound wave that is absorbed by a soft material.
☐	☐	4. <u>Interference</u> occurs when two or more waves overlap and combine to form one wave.
☐	☐	5. <u>Ultrasound</u> technology is used to create medical images and it is based on sound waves with frequencies so high that human ears cannot hear them.

Key Concepts

Read each question below, and circle the best answer.

6. Which statement best describes how humans hear sound?

   A. Sound waves enter the ear canal and increase in amplitude, which causes you to hear the sound.

   B. Sound waves cause parts of the ear to vibrate until the waves are converted to electrical signals, which are sent to the brain.

   C. Sound waves travel into people ears, then the eardrum sends the sound waves to the brain.

   D. Sound waves become sounds when they strike the eardrum inside the ear.

7. When Consuelo struck a tuning fork and held it close to a string on a guitar, the string began to vibrate on its own and make a sound. Which statement best explains why the string vibrated without anyone touching it?

   A. The string vibrated because of destructive inference between its sound waves and those of the tuning fork.

   B. The tuning fork produced ultrasonic frequencies beyond human hearing.

   C. The tuning fork and the guitar string both created mechanical waves.

   D. The string vibrated because of resonance, which happened because the tuning fork and guitar string have the same natural frequency.

8. The diagram below shows a sound wave traveling through a medium.

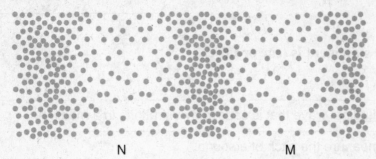

Which statement best describes how the sound wave is moving through a medium?

A. The sound wave is creating tensions and accumulations in the medium.

B. The sound wave is creating an echo inside the medium.

C. The sound wave is creating compressions and rarefactions in the medium.

D. The sound wave is creating a mechanical wave in the medium.

9. Which material best absorbs sound waves in a room?

A. heavy curtains   C. brick walls

B. hardwood floors   D. cement floors

10. Yorgos drew a diagram of a wave and labeled its parts, as shown below.

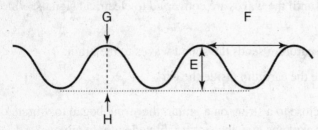

Wavelength is typically measured between the crests to two successive waves. Which labels represent a crest and a wavelength?

A. G points to a crest, F is a wavelength

B. G points to a crest, E is a wavelength

C. H points to a crest, E is a wavelength

D. H points to a crest, F is a wavelength

11. Which of the following is not a way in which echolocation is used?

A. flying bats avoiding trees and houses at night

B. sending messages over telephone lines

C. dolphins finding fish in deep water

D. mapping the ocean floor

12. Josh observed a bolt of lightning during a thunderstorm. It took more than 15 seconds for Josh to hear the sound of thunder. Why did Josh see the lighting strike before he heard the thunder?

A. Thunder always takes 15 seconds to travel through the air after lighting strikes.

B. Light waves from the lightning and sound waves from the thunder moved through different media.

C. Light waves are electromagnetic waves that travel much faster than mechanical waves, such as the sound waves he heard as thunder.

D. The conditions in the air at the time allowed light waves to move faster than the sound waves he heard as thunder.

13. The diagram below shows the distribution of particles in two different kinds of media.

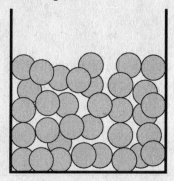 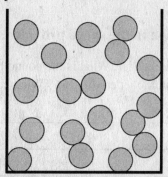

Which statement best compares how sound waves travel through the media shown above?

A. Sound waves travel at the same speed through both of the media shown.

B. Sound waves move faster through the closely packed medium on the left than the loosely packed medium on the right.

C. Sound waves move faster through the loosely packed medium on the right than the closely packed medium on the left.

D. Sound waves cannot travel through either medium that is shown above.

Critical Thinking
Answer the following questions in the space provided.

14. Describe where the cochlea is located, what parts it contains, and explain the role these parts play in human hearing.

_____

_____

_____

15. Suppose you are at a train station. What changes would you hear in the sound of the whistle as a train comes toward you and then moves away? What causes the changes, and what is this effect called?

_____

_____

_____

_____

Connect ESSENTIAL QUESTIONS

Lessons 1 and 2

Answer the following question in the space provided.

16. A fighter jet breaks the sound barrier. What is the sound barrier, and how can a jet break through it? Where does the sound around the jet come from? What causes the sonic boom, and how can you hear it?

_____

_____

_____

_____

_____

Sound

Key Concepts
Choose the letter of the best answer.

1. A few boys are sledding on snow in their favorite park. They notice that it is harder to hear someone shouting from the top of the hill to the bottom than it is in the summertime. What factor is most likely affecting the sound of their shouting?

   A. altitude

   B. frequency

   C. pressure

   D. temperature

2. The diagram below shows a sound wave traveling through air.

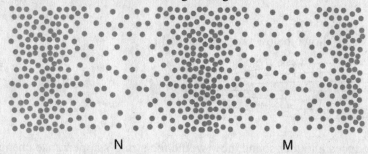

   Which terms best describes points N and M as the wave progresses?

   A. crests

   B. troughs

   C. rarefactions

   D. compressions

3. Which of the following is the best example of resonance?

   A. a bat uses ultrasonic waves to locate its next meal

   B. a telephone changes sound waves into electric signals

   C. a guitar body vibrates from the sound of a plucked string

   D. a jet produces a sonic boom as it breaks the sound barrier

4. What role does the inner ear play in hearing?

   A. captures sound waves

   B. transmits sound waves from air to fluids

   C. converts sound waves into electrical signals

   D. removes high and low sound waves that are harmful

5. Which of the following accurately describes a difference between an audio CD and a digital file?

   A. Sounds can be stored on an audio CD but not in a digital file.

   B. Unlike a digital file, an audio CD does not require a computer to record and play back sound.

   C. An audio CD stores sounds as pits on the CD's surface, whereas a digital CD stores sounds as computer code.

   D. Unlike the information stored on an audio CD, the information stored in a digital file can be converted into sound waves.

6. The vibrating guitar string shown below produces a sound.

   If the same string produced a louder sound, how would the string's appearance change?

   A. The string would vibrate to a lower height.

   B. The string would vibrate to a greater height.

   C. The string would vibrate over a longer distance.

   D. The string would vibrate over a shorter distance.

7. Two police cars are driving down the highway at 80 km/h in pursuit of a car thief. The first car turns on its siren, which has a frequency of 650 Hz. What frequency will the police officer in the second car hear?

   A. 650 Hz

   B. less than 650 Hz

   C. greater than 650 Hz

   D. There is not enough information to answer this question.

8. For what purpose do bats use ultrasonic waves?

   A. sonar

   B. ultrasound

   C. echolocation

   D. Doppler effects

9. What part of the telephone is responsible for converting sound waves into electrical signals?

   A. switch

   B. wall jack

   C. microphone

   D. speaker

10. A sound wave travels through air at a speed of 350 m/s. Which of the following most likely describes the speed of that sound wave through water?

   A. 350 m/s

   B. less than 350 m/s

   C. greater than 350 m/s

   D. There is not enough information to answer this question.

11. A game show is creating soundproof booths for contestants. Which material should be used on the walls inside the booth?

   A. wood panels

   B. wedged foam

   C. stainless steel plates

   D. nothing

12. Which of the following shows the destructive interference of two transverse waves?

A.

B.

C.

D.

Critical Thinking

Answer the following questions in the space provided.

13. Martin is measuring the speed of sound through different temperatures of water. What should he expect his findings to show? Explain your answer.

_____

_____

_____

_____

Extended Response

Answer the following questions in the space provided.

14. A man is deciding between three separate alarm systems to install in his home. Each alarm system produces a wave with a different wavelength and decibel level, as shown in the following table.

	Wavelength (cm)	Decibels (dB)
Alarm A	8	100
Alarm B	32	80
Alarm C	128	60

If the man wants the alarm with the highest pitch, which alarm should he choose? Explain your answer.

_____

_____

_____

If the man wants the loudest alarm, which alarm should he choose? Explain your answer.

_____

_____

_____

Sound

Key Concepts
Choose the letter of the best answer.

1. A couple attends an outdoor symphony in July and again in December. During the second performance, they both notice a delay in the sound, which gives the impression that they are listening to a recording rather than a live performance. What principle of the speed of sound best explains their observations?

    A. The speed of a sound wave varies with its wavelength and frequency.

    B. The speed of a sound wave depends upon the temperature of its medium.

    C. The speed of a sound wave is affected by the state of matter of the medium.

    D. The speed of a sound wave changes depending on the density of the particles in the medium.

2. The diagram below shows a sound wave traveling through air.

    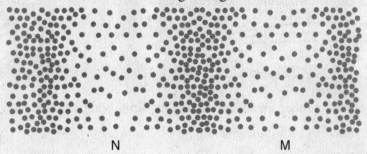

    What happens to the particles of the medium as the energy of the wave moves from point N to point M?

    A. The particles grow larger and then smaller.

    B. The particles move from point N to point M.

    C. The particles move from point M to point N.

    D. The particles move together and then apart again.

3. Which of the following is the best example of resonance?

    A. A singer holds a high-pitched note, causing a crystal glass to vibrate until it shatters.

    B. Sound waves directed into a cave strike the cave's rear wall, reflecting back to their source.

    C. A doctor sends ultrasonic waves into a person's body, producing an image of the person's internal organs.

    D. Two sound waves of nearly equal frequency interfere, producing an alternating pattern of loud and soft sounds.

4. What role does the outer ear play in hearing?

A. captures sound waves

B. transmits sound waves from air to fluids

C. converts sound waves into electrical signals

D. removes high and low sound waves that are harmful

5. Which of the following accurately describes a similarity between an audio CD and a digital file?

A. Both devices can preserve sound waves for many years.

B. Both devices prevent sound waves from losing energy over time.

C. Both devices primarily store sounds in the form of computer code.

D. Both devices store information that can be converted into sound waves.

6. The vibrating guitar string shown below produces a sound.

If the same string produced a softer sound, how would the string's appearance change?

A. The string would vibrate to a lower height.

B. The string would vibrate to a greater height.

C. The string would vibrate over a longer distance.

D. The string would vibrate over a shorter distance.

7. Two police cars are driving down a highway in pursuit of a car thief. The first car is traveling at 80 km/h; it turns on its siren, which has a frequency of 650 Hz. The second car is traveling at 75 km/h. What frequency will the police officer in the second car hear?

   A. 650 Hz

   B. less than 650 Hz

   C. greater than 650 Hz

   D. There is not enough information to answer this question.

8. What kind of waves do bats use for echolocation?

   A. infrared waves

   B. ultrasonic waves

   C. transverse waves

   D. electromagnetic waves

9. Which of the following best explains how a microphone works in a telephone?

   A. The microphone increases the volume of incoming sounds.

   B. The microphone transfers electrical signals from the wall to the phone.

   C. The microphone converts incoming sound waves into electrical signals.

   D. The microphone converts incoming electrical signals into sound waves.

10. A sound wave travels through water at a speed of 1,500 m/s. Which of the following most likely describes the speed of that sound wave through air?

    A. 1,500 m/s

    B. less than 1,500 m/s

    C. greater than 1,500 m/s

    D. There isn't enough information to answer this question.

11. A woman is building a small recording studio in her home. Which material should she cover the walls of the studio with to improve the quality of her recordings?

    A. wood panels

    B. wedged foam

    C. stainless steel plates

    D. nothing

12. Which of the following shows the constructive interference of two transverse waves?

A.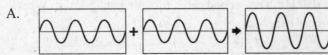

B.

C.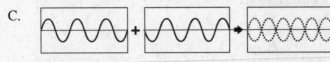

D.

Critical Thinking
Answer the following questions in the space provided.

13. Sarah is measuring the speed of sound through different states of water. What should she expect her findings to show? Explain your answer.

_____

_____

_____

_____

Extended Response
Answer the following questions in the space provided.

14. A woman is deciding between three separate alarm systems to install in her home. Each alarm system produces a wave with a different wavelength and decibel level, as shown in the following table.

	Wavelength (cm)	Decibels (dB)
Alarm A	8	100
Alarm B	32	80
Alarm C	128	60

If the woman wants the alarm with the lowest pitch, which alarm should she choose? Explain your answer.

_____

_____

_____

Based on the data in the table, which alarm produces sound waves with the greatest amplitude? Explain your answer.

_____

_____

_____

Light

Choose the letter of the best answer.

1. Energy from the sun arrives as electromagnetic radiation with a wide range of wavelengths and frequencies. Which form of electromagnetic radiation has more energy than visible light waves?

   A. microwaves

   B. radio waves

   C. infrared waves

   D. ultraviolet waves

2. The energy generated by the sun travels to Earth as electromagnetic waves of varying lengths. Which statement describes an electromagnetic wave with a long wavelength?

   A. It has a high frequency and low energy.

   B. It has a high frequency and high energy.

   C. It has a low frequency and can travel through a vacuum.

   D. It has a low frequency and needs a medium to travel through.

3. The image below shows a mirror reflecting light.

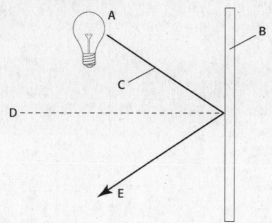

   What type of mirror is shown at label B?

   A. flat mirror

   B. convex mirror

   C. diverging mirror

   D. converging mirror

4. The diagram below shows four thin beams of light interacting with a material.

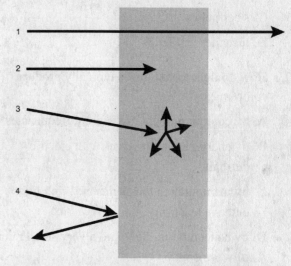

   Which beam best shows scattering?

   A. 1

   B. 2

   C. 3

   D. 4

5. Which of the following explains why the brain is important to sight?

   A. The brain controls the voluntary action of blinking.

   B. The brain turns images from the eyes into electric impulses we recognize.

   C. The brain is not important to sight; all of the necessary information comes from the eyes.

   D. The brain interprets signals from the eyes and gives us information about shape, color, and size.

6. Which of the following light technologies is known for losing very little light during transmission?

   A. LED lights

   B. laser lights

   C. fiber optics

   D. incandescent bulbs

7. How do light technologies typically produce color images?

   A. by combining light of different frequencies

   B. by energizing light waves with electric currents

   C. by manipulating the angles at which light enters a lens

   D. by concentrating light into a very small range of wavelength

8. The diagram below shows the eye, with several features labeled.

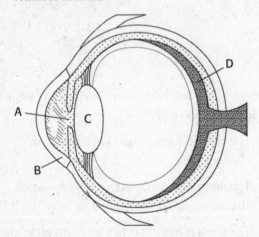

   Which part of the eye controls how much light enters the eye?

   A. A

   B. B

   C. C

   D. D

9. Three students shine lights onto the same spot on a white table. One student shines a blue light. Another student shines a red light. The third student shines a green light. What color will the spot appear to be?

   A. black

   B. orange

   C. white

   D. yellow

10. How is the shape of a diverging mirror different from the shape of a diverging lens?

   A. There is no difference; both are always convex.

   B. There is no difference; both are always concave.

   C. A diverging mirror is convex and a diverging lens is usually concave.

   D. A diverging mirror is concave and a diverging lens is usually convex.

The Electromagnetic Spectrum

Choose the letter of the best answer.

1. Electromagnetic radiation is energy that travels in waves. Two types of electromagnetic waves are infrared waves and ultraviolet waves. Which of these statements describes a property that is shared by infrared waves and ultraviolet waves?

   A. Both waves have the same energy.

   B. Both waves have the same frequency.

   C. Both waves have the same wavelength.

   D. Both waves travel at the same speed in a vacuum.

2. Electromagnetic energy travels through space in waves. The electromagnetic spectrum includes all electromagnetic waves, arranged according to frequency and wavelength. Which of these is an example of an electromagnetic wave?

   A. radio wave

   B. sound wave

   C. ocean wave

   D. gravitational pull

3. The diagram below shows a wave. The features of the wave are labeled A, B, C, and D.

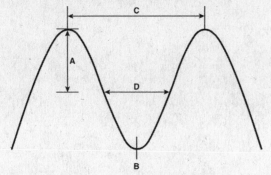

   Which label identifies the wavelength?

   A. A

   B. B

   C. C

   D. D

4. The visible part of the electromagnetic spectrum consists of the colors that we see in a rainbow. Different colors correspond to different wavelengths of light. Which color of visible light has the shortest wavelength?

   A. red

   B. green

   C. violet

   D. yellow

5. Imagine a scientist detects an electromagnetic wave with a higher frequency than that of most gamma-ray waves. The scientist calls these waves delta rays. Which of these statements would be true of delta rays?

   A. Delta rays would travel faster than most gamma rays.

   B. Delta rays would have more energy than most gamma rays do.

   C. Delta rays would have the same wavelength as most gamma rays.

   D. Delta rays would have a longer wavelength than most gamma rays have.

Interactions of Light

Choose the letter of the best answer.

1. Which of these materials best scatters the light that strikes it?

   A. pure water

   B. shiny mirror

   C. frosted glass

   D. eyeglass lens

2. The diagram below shows four thin beams of light interacting with a material.

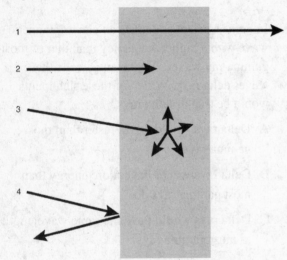

   Which beam best shows absorption?

   A. 1

   B. 2

   C. 3

   D. 4

3. Which color will a red rose appear to be if only a blue light reached it?

   A. red

   B. white

   C. black

   D. purple

4. In which of these situations would light slow down?

   A. from glass to air

   B. from ice to water

   C. from plastic to air

   D. from a vacuum to air

5. Sunlight contains all visible wavelengths of light. Each wavelength is a different color. When sunlight passes into and out of a raindrop, the light rays bend. Which color of light bends the most?

   A. blue

   B. green

   C. orange

   D. red

Mirrors and Lenses

Choose the letter of the best answer.

1. Which type of mirror causes beams of light to spread apart?

   A. flat mirror

   B. concave mirror

   C. diverging mirror

   D. converging mirror

2. The diagram below shows a flat mirror reflecting light.

   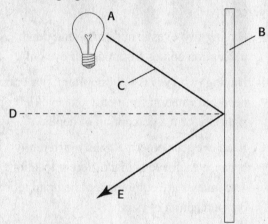

   In the above image, what is represented by line D?

   A. the mirror

   B. the angle of reflected light

   C. the angle at which light hits the surface of the mirror

   D. the imaginary line used to measure angles of rays

3. As you are shopping in your favorite store, you look up and notice a convex mirror in the corner. What type of mirror is this and what is most likely its purpose?

   A. It's a converging mirror and it's used to magnify light in the store.

   B. It's a diverging mirror and it's used to show a large area of the store.

   C. It's a diverging mirror and it's used to produce a bright beam of light.

   D. It's a converging mirror and it's used to show a large area of the store.

4. A student has noticed that she can't see objects clearly when they are far away. An eye doctor diagnoses her as being nearsighted. What type of lens could help the student correct her vision problem?

   A. flat lens

   B. convex lens

   C. diverging lens

   D. converging lens

5. A ray of light hits a mirror at a 45 degree angle. Which of the following statements is true about the way the light will reflect off the mirror?

   A. The light will not reflect off the mirror.

   B. The light will reflect at a 45 degree angle.

   C. The light will reflect at a 90 degree angle.

   D. The light will reflect at many different angles off the mirror.

Name _____ Date _____

Light Waves and Sight

Choose the letter of the best answer.

1. The diagram below shows the eye, with several features labeled.

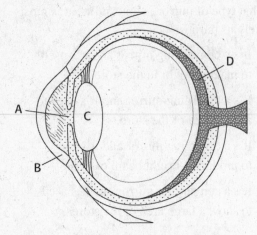

   Which part of the eye is responsible for focusing an image onto the retina?

   A. A

   B. B

   C. C

   D. D

2. After noticing changes in your vision, you take a trip to the eye doctor. She tells you that to improve your vision, she needs to perform surgery to slightly flatten the cornea. What is wrong with your eyes?

   A. They are farsighted.

   B. They are nearsighted.

   C. The retina is not functioning correctly.

   D. They cannot see objects clearly up close.

3. What type of specialized cell in the eye is used for detecting low levels of light?

   A. rod cell

   B. cone cell

   C. blood cell

   D. stem cell

4. Which of the following statements best explains the relationship between eyes and depth perception?

   A. Having two eyes is not important; depth perception comes from our left eye only.

   B. Having two eyes is not important; our brains need information from only one eye (left or right) to form a perception of depth.

   C. Each eye sees objects slightly differently because each eye is in a different location. The images are combined in the brain to form our perception of depth.

   D. One eye sees objects at a close distance, and the other eye sees objects located far away. The images are combined in the brain to form our perception of depth.

5. Which of the following is a characteristic of farsighted eyes?

   A. cannot see clearly at any distance

   B. can see things up close most clearly

   C. cannot see things clearly at a distance

   D. can see things most clearly at a distance

Light Technology

Choose the letter of the best answer.

1. Which of the following is an example of a way that light can transmit information?

   A. eyeglasses

   B. neon lights

   C. laser welder

   D. bar code scanner

2. What is one of the earliest ways that ancient peoples produced light?

   A. candles

   B. light emitting diodes

   C. fluorescent bulbs

   D. incandescent bulbs

3. A scientist is studying great horned owls. Which of the following technologies would most help the scientist observe the birds from a distance?

   A. binoculars

   B. microscope

   C. laser scanner

   D. light-emitting diode screen

4. How do incandescent bulbs produce light?

   A. Light of one color is concentrated and amplified.

   B. Material inside the bulb becomes hot and produces light.

   C. Gases within the bulb are energized by an electric current and interact with a phosphor coating.

   D. Solid materials within the bulb are energized by an electric current.

5. The following image shows one type of light technology.

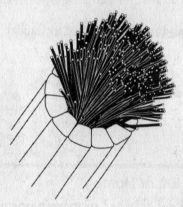

   What technology is shown above and what is one of its uses?

   A. laser; cutting through metal

   B. LED; illuminating a television screen

   C. fluorescent light; illuminating a dark room

   D. fiber optic cable; moving light through small openings

The Electromagnetic Spectrum

Climb the Ladder: *Bright Ideas*
Select activities to show what you've learned about electromagnetic waves and their properties.

1. Work on your own, with a partner, or with a small group.

2. Choose one item from each rung of the ladder. Check your choices.

3. Have your teacher approve your plan.

4. Submit or present your results.

__ EM at Home	__ Light and Stars
Find out how two or three types of electromagnetic waves are used in everyday life. Make a poster indicating the waves and their wavelengths and showing their applications at home, in school, in health care, and other settings.	Find out how scientists have used their understanding of light, color, and energy to determine the temperatures of stars. Show what you learn in a diagram or illustration.
__ A Colorful Performance	__ Found Prisms
Develop a skit that explains how the color of visible light is related to its wavelength. Perform your skit for the class and be ready to answer questions afterwards.	Find a household object that will act like a prism and separate white light into its component colors. Give a presentation to show your class how your home-grown prism works and explain the differences among the colors that you see.
__ Make a Table	__ Make a Concept Map
Make a table that lists examples of each of the different types of EM waves making up the EM spectrum. You might include columns that tell the wavelength, frequency, and energy for each type. Choose an order to present your information, such as increasing wavelength or decreasing energy.	Develop a concept map about the electromagnetic spectrum. Use words and images to express ideas and concepts that are important to understand.

Interactions of Light

Points of View: *Light*
**Complete the activities to show what you've learned about
light and the way it interacts with matter.**

1. Work in groups as assigned by your teacher. Each group will be assigned to one or two viewpoints.

2. Complete your assignment, and present your perspective to the class.

 Terms The words *absorb*, *reflect*, *refract*, *media*, and *scatter* all relate to light. Write a short story that tells what happens to a group of light beams that leave the sun, enter Earth's atmosphere, and interact with different media, such as water and grass.

 Examples List examples of three objects that reflect light, three objects that scatter light, and three objects that transmit light. Tell the characteristics common to all three objects in each group.

 Analysis Imagine that at a museum, you walk by a display of silhouettes that are lit with yellow light. Your yellow and white shirt appears to be solid yellow. Tell why.

 Observations Fill a clear glass with water. Set the glass on a table or desk to look at it from the side. Put a pencil in the water at an angle. What is strange about the way the pencil looks? What is causing the pencil to look this way?

 Details When a single light source (such as a lamp) is used in an otherwise dark room, the light spreads out and fills the room. Explain why a single lamp can help light a whole room. Tell what happens to the light when it encounters a glass of water, a metal file cabinet, and a filmy window curtain.

Mirrors and Lenses

Mix and Match: *Reflecting and Refracting Light*

Mix and match ideas to show what you've learned about how mirrors and lenses form images.

1. Work on your own, with a partner, or with a small group.

2. Choose one information source from Column A, two topics from Column B, and one option from Column C. Check your choices.

3. Have your teacher approve your plan.

4. Submit or present your results.

A. Choose One Information Source	B. Choose Two Things to Analyze	C. Choose One Way to Communicate Analysis
___ Internet article about lenses and/or mirrors	___ plane mirrors	___ mural or poster
___ library book about science projects using lenses and/or mirrors	___ concave mirrors	___ photos using computerized special effects, such as mirrors or convex and concave lenses
___ interactive activity demonstrating how a mirror reflects light and/or how a lens bends light	___ convex mirrors	___ website for younger students explaining how mirrors and lenses work
___ observations of mirrors and/or lenses	___ concave lenses	___ model, such as funhouse mirrors
___ diagram explaining how a telescope, magnifying glass, pair of eyeglasses, camera, or other tool or device operates using mirrors and/or lenses	___ convex lenses	___ story, song, or poem, with supporting details
		___ skit, chant, or dance, with supporting details
_____		___ multimedia presentation
		_____

Light Waves and Sight

Mix and Match: *The Eye-Brain Connection*

Mix and match ideas to show what you've learned about how the eye and the brain work together to make vision possible.

1. Work on your own, with a partner, or with a small group.

2. Choose one information source from Column A, all of Column B, and one option from Column C.

3. Check your choices.

4. Have your teacher approve your plan.

5. Submit or present your results.

A. Choose One Information Source	B. Include Each of These Things	C. Choose One Way to Communicate Your Understanding
___ observations of a normal eye and an eye with vision problems ___ video of an eye surgery ___ a medical website that describes vision ___ a book about vision _____	___ the eye's role in vision ___ the brain's role in vision ___ a description of a common vision problem and how it is corrected	___ diagram or illustration ___ model, such as drawings or descriptions connected by strings ___ booklet, such as a medical brochure ___ game ___ story, song, or poem, with supporting details ___ skit, chant, or dance, with supporting details ___ multimedia presentation _____

Light Technology

Take Your Pick: *Making Light Work*

1. Work on your own or with a partner.

2. Choose items below for a total of 10 points. Check your choices.

3. Have your teacher approve your plan.

4. Submit or present your results.

2 Points

_____ **Comparing** Make a sketch that shows how a laser light is different from the light beam of a flashlight.

_____ **Name a Tool** Write a paragraph that names one optical tool, describes how it works, and explains how it is used.

_____ **Identifying Relationships** Draw a Venn Diagram to compare fluorescent and LED bulbs.

5 Points

_____ **Draw a Poster** Draw a poster that explains the concept of total internal reflection.

_____ **Doppler Radar** Design a weather report for your town that includes the use of Doppler radar.

_____ **Calculate Distance** How can the speed of light and a laser beam be used to measure the distance between two satellites? Sketch your ideas.

8 Points

_____ **Lasers and Nanotechnology** Learn more about how lasers are having a big impact on nanotechnology. Pick one interesting development and research that topic. Share your findings with the class through a short multimedia or oral presentation.

_____ **Design a Pinhole Camera** Use research materials or the Internet to design a pinhole camera. List the materials you will need. Write the steps for how to put it together. Explain how the camera will take pictures.

Arranging the Electromagnetic Spectrum

Purpose Students will place the various regions of the electromagnetic spectrum in the correct order, beginning with the region of lowest energy and moving in the direction of increasing energy.

Time Period 20 minutes

Preparation Make copies of the diagram of the electromagnetic spectrum. The diagram should not contain wavelengths or other features that help students identify the order. Then cut the pieces into seven labeled sections: radiowaves, microwaves, infrared, visible light, ultraviolet, X-rays, and Gamma rays. Be sure each pair of students has one copy of each section.

Teaching Strategies This activity works best when carried out by pairs of students.

Scoring Rubric

Possible points	Performance indicators
0–20	Appropriate use of materials and equipment
0–40	Quality of spectrum assembly and sketch
0–40	Quality of answers to questions

Arranging the Electromagnetic Spectrum

Objective

In this activity, you will cut out sections of paper representing different regions of the electromagnetic spectrum. You will place the regions in order from lowest energy to highest energy.

Know the Score!

As you work through this activity, keep in mind that you will be earning a grade for the following:

- how well you work with materials and equipment (20%)
- how well you arrange the regions and put together the sketch of your results (40%)
- how well you answer questions (40%)

Materials and Equipment

- paper copies representing sections within the electromagnetic spectrum

Procedure

1. Arrange the sections in order from left to right, with the lowest energy waves at the far left and the highest energy waves at the far right.

2. Draw a sketch of your arrangement below.

Analysis

3. How does wavelength change as you go from left to right along your spectrum?

_____

_____

_____

4. How does frequency change as you go from left to right along your spectrum?

    _____

    _____

    _____

5. Why were the paper cutouts for each region of the spectrum made to have different widths?

    _____

    _____

    _____

6. Which regions of the electromagnetic spectrum are detectable by humans? Explain.

    _____

    _____

    _____

Unit 3: Light

Vocabulary

Check the box to show whether each statement is true or false.

T	F	
☐	☐	1. A <u>convex</u> mirror curves outward like the back of a spoon.
☐	☐	2. <u>Laser</u> light is more intense than other types of light because it comes from a very small range of wavelengths in the visible spectrum.
☐	☐	3. Electromagnetic waves travel through a medium by <u>radiation</u>.
☐	☐	4. <u>Scattering</u> occurs when certain wavelengths of light are reflected by particles, causing the light to spread out in all directions
☐	☐	5. A material that allows light to pass through it completely is <u>transparent</u>.

Key Concepts

Read each question below, and circle the best answer.

6. Which statement best explains why most people can see colors?

   A. The eyes and brain can see all wavelengths in the electromagnetic spectrum.

   B. The eyes and brain rely on all of the radiation from the sun to see colors.

   C. The eyes and brain interpret different wavelengths of visible light as different colors.

   D. The eyes and brain see light waves only when they travel through a medium.

7. What type of cells in the retina are involved in detecting light?

   A. the lens and the cornea

   B. rod cells and lenses

   C. rod cells and cone cells

   D. cone cells and corneas

8. The table below lists electromagnetic waves.

Low frequency

A	B	C	D
Radio waves	Gamma rays	Laser light	Visible light
Microwaves	x-rays	Visible light	x-rays
Infrared waves	Ultraviolet light	Ultraviolet light	Ultraviolet light
Visible light	Visible light	x-rays	Radio waves
Ultraviolet light	Infrared light	Gamma rays	Microwaves

High frequency

Which column correctly lists waves from lowest to highest frequencies?

A. Column A

B. Column B

C. Column C

D. Column D

9. Which statement best tells the ways in which light interacts with matter?

A. Light can come from the sun, fire, or a light bulb.

B. Light waves can be reflected, refracted, or absorbed by matter.

C. Laser light goes through matter, and all other light gets stopped by matter.

D. Only visible light can interact with matter.

10. Waves of red light and yellow light go through air and strike a piece of glass. The diagram shows how the two kinds of light interact with the glass.

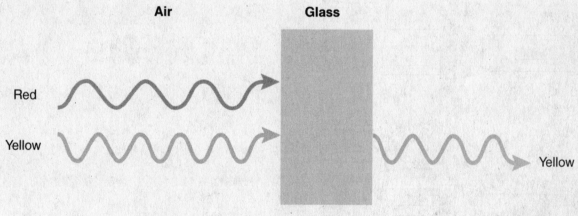

Which statement describes how the glass interacts with red and yellow light?

A. The glass absorbs red light and transmits yellow light.

B. The glass transmits red light and absorbs yellow light.

C. The glass reflects both red and yellow light.

D. The glass transmits both red and yellow light.

11. A beam of incoming light strikes a flat mirror. The mirror reflects the light.

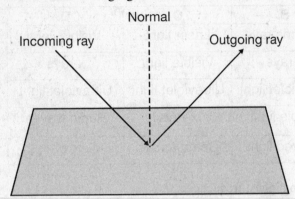

Which statement best explains what this diagram of a light ray and a mirror is showing?

A. A mirror scatters most of the light that strikes its surface.

B. The normal absorbs rays of light that strike the surface of a mirror.

C. The normal measures the angle of a light ray reflecting off the surface of a flat mirror.

D. The angle of an incoming ray is used to predict the angle of the normal when light strikes the surface.

12. When Juan shined a light through the liquid in glass A then glass B, he saw that the liquids in the two glasses looked different.

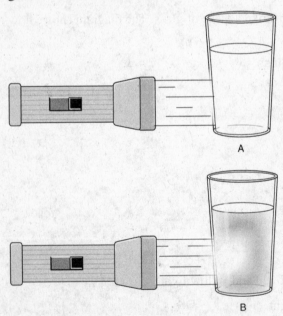

What did the liquids' appearance tell about how light was interacting with them?

A. The liquid in glass A absorbed light, the liquid in glass B reflected light.

B. The liquid in glass A was transparent, the liquid in glass B was translucent.

C. The liquid in glass A was translucent, the liquid in glass be was transparent.

D. The liquids looked different because the liquid in glass A scattered more light than the liquid in glass B.

13. The electromagnetic spectrum includes all electromagnetic waves, from radio waves with long wavelengths and low frequencies to gamma rays with short wavelengths and high frequencies. Which statement best describes how fast these waves travel in a vacuum?

    A. Gamma rays travel much faster than others because they have the highest frequencies.

    B. High frequency waves travel somewhat faster than low frequency waves

    C. Infrared waves travel faster than ultraviolet waves.

    D. All electromagnetic waves travel at the same speed.

Critical Thinking
Answer the following questions in the space provided.

14. Explain what the cornea is and how it interacts with light. What is the role of the retina in vision?

    _____

    _____

15. Name three main shapes that mirrors can have. What is the difference between converging and diverging mirrors? Describe real and virtual images.

    _____

    _____

    _____

    _____

    _____

Connect ESSENTIAL QUESTIONS

Lessons 1, 4, and 5

Answer the following question in the space provided.

16. Give two examples of natural light and two examples of artificial light. How is natural light transmitted? How is artificial light produced?

    _____

    _____

    _____

    _____

    _____

Light

Key Concepts
Choose the letter of the best answer.

1. As you walk outside, you notice a rainbow, full of many different colors. Which part of your eye helps you distinguish the different colors?

   A. pupil

   B. cornea

   C. rod cells

   D. cone cells

2. What type of light technology emits light by energizing solid particles with an electric current?

   A. LED

   B. laser

   C. incandescent

   D. No type of light is produced by energized solid particles.

3. The diagram below shows how two different viewers would see the same object in a mirror.

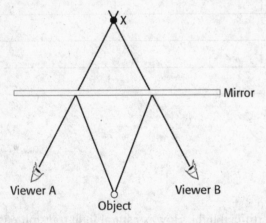

   Which of the following statements about the image, shown at label X, is true?

   A. None of the viewers can see the image.

   B. The image appears to be behind the mirror.

   C. The image appears different to each viewer.

   D. The image appears to be in front of the mirror.

4. After noticing you have trouble seeing things at a distance, your eye doctor prescribes glasses for you to wear. How is this a type of light technology?

   A. Eyeglasses can store information.

   B. Eyeglasses can transfer information.

   C. Eyeglasses can help humans control light.

   D. Eyeglasses can emit light to help us see better.

5. A student shines a thin beam of light onto a prism. The light contains wavelengths of red, blue, green, and yellow light. The diagram below shows how the four colors of light exit the prism at different angles.

   Which of the wavelengths is color 1?

   A. red light

   B. blue light

   C. green light

   D. yellow light

6. What happens when parallel beams of light strike a converging mirror?

   A. They all reflect to a single focal point.

   B. They reflect in parallel beams.

   C. They reflect in a spread-out pattern.

   D. They form an image that appears to be behind the mirror.

7. It is foggy outside one morning. Which term best describes the fog?

   A. opaque

   B. reflective

   C. translucent

   D. transparent

8. The table below shows characteristics of vision problems and explains how these problems can be solved. Some of the information is missing.

Symptoms and solutions	Nearsightedness	Farsightedness
Symptoms	• trouble seeing at a distance • can see objects up close	• trouble seeing up close • can see objects at a distance
Corrective Lens Solution	• diverging lens	• ?
Surgery Solution	• ?	• increase curve of cornea

Which of the following best completes the table?

   A. a surgery solution for nearsightedness: enlarge the pupil; a corrective lens solution for farsightedness: contact lens

   B. a surgery solution for nearsightedness: flatten the cornea; a corrective lens solution for farsightedness: contact lens

   C. a surgery solution for nearsightedness: enlarge the pupil; a corrective lens solution for farsightedness: converging lens

   D. a surgery solution for nearsightedness: flatten the cornea; a corrective lens solution for farsightedness: converging lens

9. Which of the following statements about reflected images is true?

   A. Reflected images are always virtual images.

   B. Reflected images can vary in many ways from the actual object.

   C. Reflected images always look slightly bigger than the actual object.

   D. Reflected images always look exactly like the object they are reflecting.

10. The following graph lists the range of wavelengths for several kinds of light.

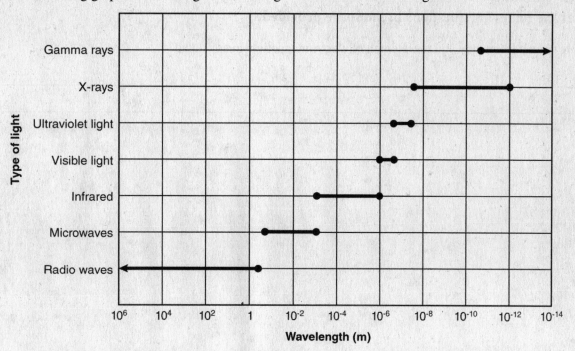

Which of the waves listed below has the highest frequency?

A. radio waves

B. x-ray waves

C. infrared waves

D. ultraviolet waves

11. What happens to light images once they are in the retina?

A. Our eyes blink.

B. The retina interprets the images.

C. The images are sent to the brain.

D. The images are sent to the cornea.

12. What is electromagnetic radiation?

A. a magnetic field

B. the transfer of energy as sound waves

C. the transfer of energy as electromagnetic waves

D. the medium through which electromagnetic waves travel

Critical Thinking

Answer the following questions in the space provided.

13. How are the frequency and wavelength of electromagnetic waves related?

_____

_____

Extended Response

Answer the following questions in the space provided.

14. If you have a red backpack, what color would it appear if you look at it through red glass? What color would the backpack appear if you look at it through blue glass? Explain your answer.

_____

_____

_____

_____

_____

Light

Key Concepts
Choose the letter of the best answer.

1. Why are cone cells important for seeing something like a rainbow?

   A. Cone cells help us distinguish colors.

   B. Cone cells help us determine distance.

   C. Cone cells reflect light.

   D. Cone cells detect low-light levels.

2. How do LED lights differ from fluorescent lights?

   A. LEDs emit light because of heat; fluorescent bulbs emit light because of energized solids.

   B. LEDs emit light by concentrating wavelengths of light; fluorescent bulbs emit light because of heat.

   C. LEDs emit light because of energized solids; fluorescent bulbs emit light because UV light interacts with a phosphor coating.

   D. LEDs emit light because UV light interacts with a phosphor coating; fluorescent bulbs emit light by concentrating wavelengths of light.

3. The diagram below shows how two different viewers would see the same object in a mirror.

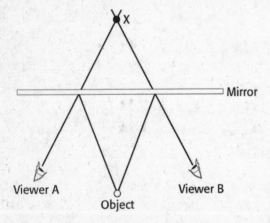

   In the diagram above, what is represented by the label X?

   A. a real image of the object

   B. a virtual image of the object

   C. a magnified image of the object

   D. an image of the two different viewers

4. Which of the following is an example of a technology that uses light to physically change matter?

   A. an oven that captures sunlight to cook food

   B. a microscope that focuses light to magnify an image

   C. optical fibers that transmit information stored as light

   D. corrective lenses that redirect light as it enters the eyes of a nearsighted person

5. A student shines a thin beam of light onto a prism. The light contains wavelengths of red, blue, green, and yellow light. The diagram below shows how the four colors of light exit the prism at different angles.

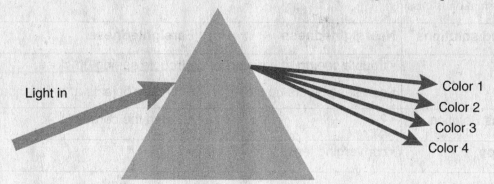

   The student then states that Color 1 is red. Which response below best explains why this is correct or incorrect?

   A. Color 1 is red because it refracts the least.

   B. Color 1 is red because it refracts the most.

   C. Color 1 is not red. Color 1 should be blue because blue refracts the least.

   D. Color 1 is not red. Color 1 should be blue because blue refracts the most.

6. A beam of light is placed at the focal point in front of a converging mirror. What will happen when the beam shines toward the mirror?

   A. The beam of light will reflect back to the focal point.

   B. The beam of light will reflect off the mirror and then diverge.

   C. The beam of light will reflect off the mirror and then form a parallel beam.

   D. Converging mirrors do not have focal points in front of the mirror; the focal point is behind the mirror.

7. A student wakes up one morning and sees that it is foggy outside. Which response below best describes what is happening to the light outside?

A. The fog scatters the light.

B. No light is transmitted at all.

C. The light bounces off the fog.

D. The light travels clearly through the fog.

8. The table below shows characteristics of vision problems and explains how these problems can be solved. Some of the information is missing.

Symptoms and solutions	Nearsightedness	Farsightedness
Symptoms	• trouble seeing at a distance • can see objects up close	• trouble seeing up close • can see objects at a distance
Corrective Lens Solution	• ?	• flatten the cornea
Surgery Solution	• converging lens	• ?

Which of the following best completes the table?

A. a corrective lens solution for nearsightedness: contact lens; a surgery solution for farsightedness: enlarge the pupil

B. a corrective lens solution for nearsightedness: contact lens; a surgery solution for farsightedness: increase the curve of the cornea

C. a corrective lens solution for nearsightedness: diverging lens; a surgery solution for farsightedness: enlarge the pupil

D. a corrective lens solution for nearsightedness: diverging lens; a surgery solution for farsightedness: increase the curve of the cornea

9. An object is placed beyond the focal point of a concave mirror (position 1). The object then moves closer to the mirror, so that the object is closer to the mirror than the focal point (position 2). Which response below best describes the types of images you will see at each position of the object?

A. 1: real image; 2: real image

B. 1: real image; 2: virtual image

C. 1: virtual image; 2: real image

D. 1: virtual image; 2: virtual image

10. The following graph lists the range of wavelengths for several kinds of light.

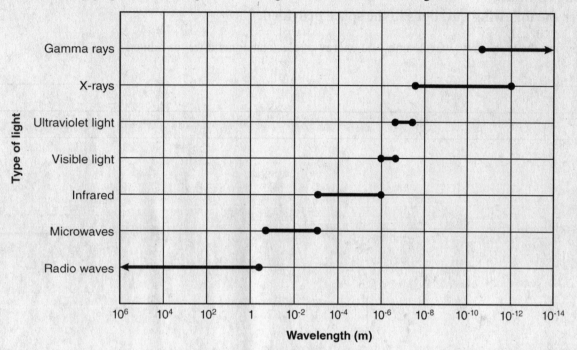

Which of the waves listed below has the shortest wavelength?

A. radio waves

B. x-ray waves

C. infrared waves

D. ultraviolet waves

11. Light enters the eye through the cornea, and then is limited through the pupil and focused through the lens. Which response below best describes where light images go next?

A. to the brain and then to the optic nerve

B. to the optic nerve and then to the front of the eye

C. to the retina and then to the brain

D. to the optic nerve and then to the retina

12. Which of the choices below is another term for the transfer of energy as electromagnetic waves?

A. medium

B. magnetic field

C. electromagnetic radiation

D. wavelength and amplitude

Critical Thinking

Answer the following questions in the space provided.

13. How are the frequency, wavelength, and energy of electromagnetic waves related?

_____

_____

_____

Extended Response
Answer the following questions in the space provided.

14. If you have a blue backpack, what color would it appear if you look at it through blue glass? What color would the backpack appear if you look at it through red glass? Explain your answer.

_____

_____

_____

_____

_____

Sound and Light

Choose the letter of the best answer.

1. An earthquake wave travels from its source underground to the ocean floor. What will happen to the wave when it meets the water in the ocean?

    A. It will stop.

    B. It will move faster.

    C. It will move slower.

    D. It will continue to move at the same speed.

2. The diagram below shows how two different viewers would see the same object in a mirror.

    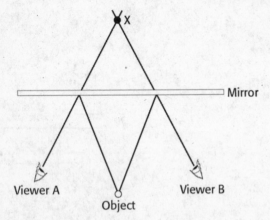

    Why does the image, shown at point X, appear to be behind the mirror?

    A. The image appears to be behind the mirror because the object is behind the mirror.

    B. The image appears to be behind the mirror because the viewers are behind the mirror.

    C. The image appears to be behind the mirror because our brains interpret light in straight lines.

    D. The image appears to be behind the mirror because the rays from the image come from behind the mirror.

3. Through which of these media do sound waves travel the fastest?

    A. rock

    B. hot air

    C. seawater

    D. foam

4. A violin string is plucked. A second string is plucked, and the sound is higher in pitch but quieter. What is different about the sound wave of the second sound compared to the first?

A. increased wavelength and decreased loudness

B. decreased frequency and increased loudness

C. increased frequency and decreased amplitude

D. decreased wavelength and increased amplitude

5. The diagram below shows a sound wave moving through air.

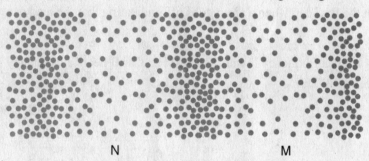

N   M

What would be different about this diagram if the sound wave were moving through a solid?

A. There would be more compressions.

B. Points N and M would be further apart.

C. There would be many more particles closely packed together.

D. Sound waves cannot pass through solids.

6. Which of the following properties is true of a converging lens?

A. is often concave on both sides

B. focuses a parallel beam to a point

C. causes a parallel beam to spread out

D. is thinner at the center than at the edge

7. Light rays enter a translucent material. Which description best describes what happens to the light rays?

A. The rays bounce straight back.

B. The rays move straight through.

C. The rays spread out in all directions.

D. The rays move through, but in one new direction.

8. Some cameras record motion data. What is the correct term for the sequence of images recorded in this way?

   A. book

   B. video

   C. photo

   D. computer

9. Three cars are competing in a race in which they must complete an unknown number of laps around a track. They are notified that they are on the final lap when a siren goes off, indicating that the lead car has begun the final lap.

   When the siren blares at 800 Hz, Car A hears a frequency lower than 800 Hz. Car B hears a frequency higher than 800 Hz. Car C hears the siren at 800 Hz.

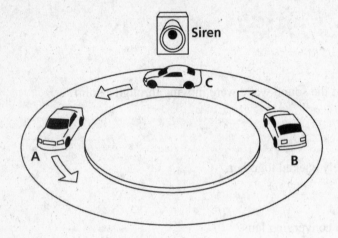

   What is the correct order of the cars?

   A. 1st Place: Car A; 2nd Place: Car B; 3rd Place: Car C

   B. 1st Place: Car B; 2nd Place: Car C; 3rd Place: Car A

   C. 1st Place: Car C; 2nd Place: Car B; 3rd Place: Car A

   D. 1st Place: Car C; 2nd Place: Car A; 3rd Place: Car B

10. When you speak into a phone, the energy in the sound you make travels from your phone to someone else's. In what form does the energy most likely travel for most of the journey?

    A. light impulses

    B. electric signals

    C. ultrasonic waves

    D. compression waves

11. The medium through which a mechanical wave passes can be a solid, a liquid, or a gas. Properties of a wave might change when it moves from one medium to another. What happens to the speed of a wave when it moves from a gas to a solid?

   A. It speeds up.

   B. It slows down.

   C. It remains the same.

   D. It speeds up and then slows down.

12. Chang noticed that it took 2 s for a wave to pass where he was swimming. What property of a wave did he measure?

   A. period

   B. speed

   C. amplitude

   D. wavelength

13. The graph below shows the motion of particles as a wave passes through a medium.

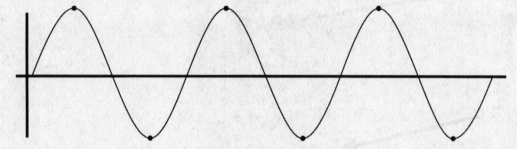

   The wave is moving along the x-axis. What type of wave is shown in the graph?

   A. medium

   B. transverse

   C. longitudinal

   D. electromagnetic

14. What is a natural frequency?

   A. the frequency at which all matter vibrates

   B. the frequency that musical instruments are tuned to

   C. the frequency at which an object vibrates

   D. the frequency of the background noise in the universe

15. Mei knows the wavelength and the frequency of a wave. How will she use this information to calculate the speed of the wave?

    A. Add frequency and wavelength.

    B. Divide frequency by wavelength.

    C. Divide wavelength by frequency.

    D. Multiply wavelength and frequency.

16. The diagram below shows four light rays interacting with a material.

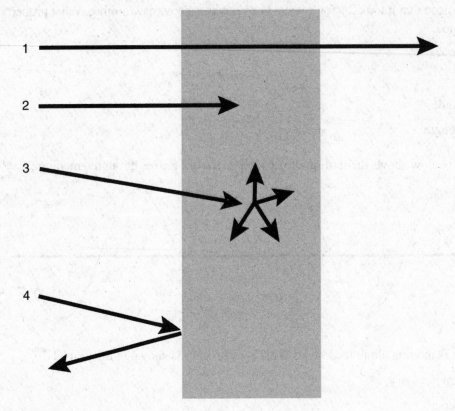

The material is transparent to which light ray?

    A. ray 1

    B. ray 2

    C. ray 3

    D. ray 4

17. How does the brain transform the two-dimensional images we receive from our eyes into the three-dimensional images we perceive?

   A. It creates three-dimensional images with the help of rod and cone cells.

   B. It selects and fills out the two-dimensional image that is closest to reality.

   C. It combines the different images from each eye to form a three-dimensional image.

   D. It creates three-dimensional images by making one eye work much harder than the other eye.

18. In which of the following scenarios would a diverging mirror most likely be used?

   A. shining a flashlight in the dark

   B. viewing stars through a telescope

   C. magnifying the image of cells in a microscope

   D. showing a wider view of a narrow, dangerous intersection

19. What vision problem can be corrected by flattening the cornea?

   A. blindness

   B. farsightedness

   C. nearsightedness

   D. color vision deficiency

20. Look at the following diagram of sound waves:

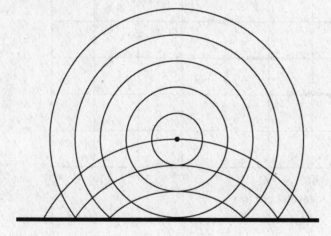

What principle of sound is being demonstrated in this diagram?

   A. Doppler effect

   B. echo

   C. resonance

   D. speed of sound

21. What is a sonic boom?

    A. the sound of air particles breaking

    B. the destructive interference of many sound waves

    C. the constructive interference of many sound waves

    D. the sound that occurs before the sound barrier is broken

22. Great amounts of electromagnetic energy from our sun and other bodies in space travel through space. Which is a logical conclusion about these electromagnetic waves?

    A. Their energy must be very low.

    B. Their frequency must be very low.

    C. Their wavelengths must be very short.

    D. These waves can travel without a medium.

23. The figure below shows the regions of the electromagnetic spectrum.

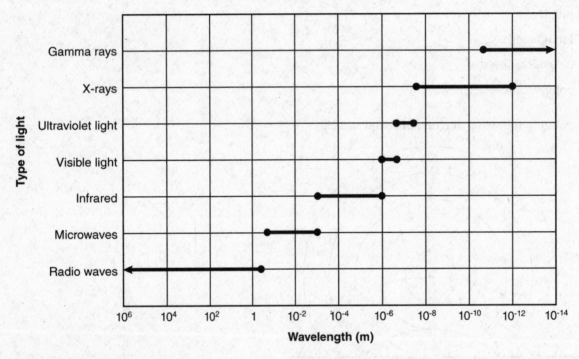

Which of these statements is **true**?

    A. X-rays are shorter than visible light waves.

    B. Ultraviolet waves are longer than radio waves.

    C. Visible light waves are longer than microwaves.

    D. Infrared waves are shorter than ultraviolet waves.

24. A jellyfish is floating in the ocean. What will happen to the jellyfish when a wave passes through the water?

    A. It will be carried away with the wave.

    B. It will be moved up to the surface of the water.

    C. It will not move, but the water around it will move.

    D. It will move up and down, but it will return to about the same place.

25. A submarine sends sonar signals to the ocean floor. Over time, the signals take longer to reflect off of the ocean floor and back to the submarine. Which of the following could explain why this is?

    A. The signals could be reflecting off of objects above the ocean floor.

    B. The sound waves could be slowing as they move through the water.

    C. The submarine could be rising toward the surface.

    D. The submarine could be moving toward the ocean floor.

26. The diagram below shows the eye, with several features labeled.

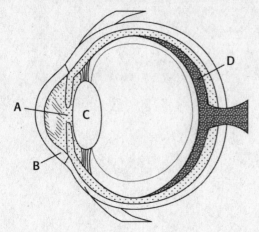

In which part of the eye would you find specialized cells called rods and cones?

    A. A

    B. B

    C. C

    D. D

27. Our eyes detect light that lies only within a small region of the electromagnetic spectrum. This region is called visible light. Which of these statements describes the visible spectrum of light as seen by the human eye?

   A. The lowest frequency appears green, and the highest frequency appears red.

   B. The lowest frequency appears red, and the highest frequency appears violet.

   C. The lowest frequency appears blue, and the highest frequency appears orange.

   D. The lowest frequency appears yellow, and the highest frequency appears green.

28. Which statement best explains why a banana is yellow?

   A. It emits yellow light.

   B. It reflects yellow light.

   C. It absorbs yellow light.

   D. It transmits yellow light.

29. Which of the following emits light when ultraviolet (UV) light interacts with a phosphor coating and is converted to visible light?

   A. laser

   B. fiber optic cable

   C. fluorescent light

   D. incandescent light

30. The following image shows one type of light technology.

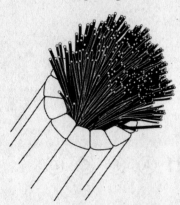

What technology is shown and how is it useful in the medical field?

A. It's an incandescent light; it can keep patients warm during surgery.

B. It's a laser; it helps doctors stay in touch with other doctors via cell phones.

C. It's a light-emitting diode; it can display information about patients on a screen.

D. It's a fiber optic cable; it can illuminate otherwise unreachable parts of the human body.

Name _____ Date _____

PLEASE NOTE

- Use only a no. 2 pencil
- Example: (A) ● (C) (D)
- Erase changes COMPLETELY.

End-of-Module Test

Mark one answer for each question.

1 (A) (B) (C) (D)   11 (A) (B) (C) (D)   21 (A) (B) (C) (D)

2 (A) (B) (C) (D)   12 (A) (B) (C) (D)   22 (A) (B) (C) (D)

3 (A) (B) (C) (D)   13 (A) (B) (C) (D)   23 (A) (B) (C) (D)

4 (A) (B) (C) (D)   14 (A) (B) (C) (D)   24 (A) (B) (C) (D)

5 (A) (B) (C) (D)   15 (A) (B) (C) (D)   25 (A) (B) (C) (D)

6 (A) (B) (C) (D)   16 (A) (B) (C) (D)   26 (A) (B) (C) (D)

7 (A) (B) (C) (D)   17 (A) (B) (C) (D)   27 (A) (B) (C) (D)

8 (A) (B) (C) (D)   18 (A) (B) (C) (D)   28 (A) (B) (C) (D)

9 (A) (B) (C) (D)   19 (A) (B) (C) (D)   29 (A) (B) (C) (D)

10 (A) (B) (C) (D)   20 (A) (B) (C) (D)   30 (A) (B) (C) (D)

Test Doctor

Unit 1 Introduction to Waves

Unit Pretest

1. C   5. B   9. D
2. B   6. A   10. B
3. C   7. B
4. A   8. B

1. C

A   is incorrect because these properties have different units and cannot be added.

B   is incorrect because the quotient has units of time/distance instead of distance/time.

C   is correct because speed is a measure of distance/time.

D   is incorrect because distance multiplied by time is not a measure of speed.

2. B

A   is incorrect because it is more than one wavelength.

B   is correct because it describes the distance between two corresponding points of a wave.

C   is incorrect because wavelength is a measure of the distance between two corresponding points of a wave.

D   is incorrect because wavelength is a measure of the distance between two corresponding points of a wave.

3. C

A   is incorrect because electromagnetic waves move at the speed of light, which is faster than any mechanical wave can travel.

B   is incorrect because electromagnetic waves are transverse waves.

C   is correct because electromagnetic waves can travel through empty space, but mechanical waves cannot.

D   is incorrect because electromagnetic waves do differ from mechanical waves.

4. A

A   is correct because sound waves move through a medium of air and ocean waves move through a medium of water.

B   is incorrect because waves do not cause permanent displacement of particles.

C   is incorrect because sound waves are produced by vibrations from vocal chords.

D   is incorrect because a wave is a transfer of energy.

5. B

A   is incorrect because a crest is the highest point of a wave.

B   is correct because a trough is the lowest point of a wave.

C   is incorrect because amplitude is the vertical distance from equilibrium, or the rest position, to either the crest or the trough.

D   is incorrect because the rest position is a point halfway between the crest and the trough.

6. A

A   is correct because mechanical waves must move through a medium, which in this case is air.

B   is incorrect because the diagram does not show the source of the wave, and mechanical waves come from a variety of sources.

C   is incorrect because waves cannot create matter.

D   is incorrect because it describes a transverse wave, which is not shown in the diagram.

7. B

A   is incorrect because the energy carried by a wave decreases with distance. The energy is spread over a greater area.

B   is correct because the energy carried by a wave decreases with distance. The energy is spread over a greater area.

C   is incorrect because the energy carried by a wave changes with distance.

D   is incorrect because the energy carried by a wave continues to decrease with distance.

8. B

A   is incorrect because a light wave is a type of electromagnetic wave.

B   is correct because a sound wave must travel through a medium and so is a mechanical wave.

C is incorrect because a gamma ray is a type of electromagnetic wave.

D is incorrect because an electromagnetic wave is not a mechanical wave.

9. D

A is incorrect because sound waves travel most quickly in a solid.

B is incorrect because sound waves travel more quickly in a liquid than in a gas.

C is incorrect because sound waves travel faster in a solid.

D is correct because sound waves travel most slowly through a gas.

10. B

A is incorrect because sound is a longitudinal wave.

B is correct because the ground moves perpendicular to the direction of the wave motion.

C is incorrect because the ground moves perpendicular, not parallel, to the direction of the wave motion.

D is incorrect because electromagnetic waves are made of vibrating electric and magnetic fields, not vibrating particles.

Lesson 1 Quiz

1. B   4. D
2. B   5. C
3. B

1. B

A is incorrect because sound waves are mechanical waves and cannot travel through empty space.

B is correct because electromagnetic waves are the only type of wave that can move through empty space.

C is incorrect because radio waves are electromagnetic waves not mechanical waves.

D is incorrect because radio waves are electromagnetic waves, or disturbances in electric and magnetic fields. They are considered transverse waves.

2. B

A is incorrect because the wave is traveling toward the door, not up and down.

B is correct because the wave moves toward the door, and the direction of the rope's motion is perpendicular to the direction of the wave motion.

C is incorrect because the wave travels along the rope.

D is incorrect because a transverse wave was produced in the rope, so the rope's motion is perpendicular to the motion of the wave.

3. B

A is incorrect because a wave is not a type of energy, even though it transfers energy.

B is correct because a wave is a disturbance that transfers energy through matter or space.

C is incorrect because a wave does not transfer matter.

D is incorrect because a wave is not a type of matter.

4. D

A is incorrect because the wave shown is a transverse wave.

B is incorrect because different kinds of waves travel at different speeds through the same medium.

C is incorrect because multiple waves can travel through a medium at the same time.

D is correct because longitudinal waves travel faster than transverse waves.

5. C

A is incorrect because an S wave is a seismic wave, not a sound wave.

B is incorrect because visible light waves are a type of electromagnetic wave.

C is correct because sound waves are a type of mechanical wave, even if humans cannot hear the sound.

D is incorrect because sound waves are not electromagnetic waves.

Lesson 2 Quiz

1. D   4. C
2. D   5. B
3. B

1. D

A is incorrect because the medium affects wave speed.

B is incorrect because mechanical waves require a medium to move at all.

C is incorrect because mechanical waves cannot travel through a vacuum.

D is correct because electromagnetic waves can

travel through a vacuum, but mechanical waves cannot.

2. D

A is incorrect because the rest position is at the center of line E.

B is incorrect because F is the wavelength.

C is incorrect because the rest position is midway between points G and H.

D is correct because the rest position is halfway between the crest and the trough.

3. B

A is incorrect because a period is measured in time.

B is correct because frequency is measured in hertz.

C is incorrect because amplitude is a distance measurement.

D is incorrect because wavelength is a distance measurement.

4. C

A is incorrect because light travels much faster than sound.

B is incorrect because sound does not travel faster than light in air.

C is correct because sound waves move faster through warmer air.

D is incorrect because sound waves move faster, not slower, through warmer air.

5. B

A is incorrect because wave energy decreases with distance.

B is correct because wave energy decreases with distance; therefore, the louder Aimee's knocking sound is, the closer she is to Patrick.

C is incorrect because sound waves travel faster in warm air than in cold air; also, a different characteristic of waves is more directly related to Aimee's knocking.

D is incorrect because although sound waves do travel faster in warm air than in cold air, a different characteristic of waves is more directly related to Aimee's knocking.

Lesson 1 Alternative Assessment

Everyday Waves: Posters show a situation in which a wave is involved, and the wave is indicated and labeled. Poster also explains whether the wave is mechanical or electromagnetic.

Making Waves: Models show both transverse and longitudinal waves, and the waves are labeled.

You Ask the Questions: Papers contain at least five questions and answers about mechanical waves.

Helping a Friend: Dialogues include the definition of a wave and describe how a wave is different from its medium.

The Wave Game: Students create eight game cards (one for each wave listed) and put each type of wave in the correct category (electromagnetic or mechanical).

Paragraph Paraphrase: Students paraphrase information

about electromagnetic waves, including the most important information from the lesson.

Which Wave Are You?: Skits show the differences and similarities between transverse and longitudinal waves. Actors talk about the characteristics of the waves, and they act out the motions of the waves.

Compare and Contrast Waves: Presentations compare and contrast mechanical and electromagnetic waves. Presentations also give examples of both types of waves.

Lesson 2 Alternative Assessment

Make a Graph: Graph shows two full wave cycles of a transverse wave that has an amplitude of 2 cm and a wavelength of 10 cm. Graph is labeled.

Make a Model: Models show two full wave cycles of a transverse wave that has an amplitude of 10 cm and a wavelength of 25 cm.

Make a Diagram: Diagrams show two full wave cycles of a transverse wave that has an amplitude of 20 cm and a wavelength of 30 cm.

Calculate Speed: Calculations show wave speeds for one of the waves listed above, for four periods.

Design a Poster: Posters explain what wave speed is and what factors play a role in determining wave speed for both mechanical and electromagnetic waves.

Concept Map: Concept maps explain how amplitude, wavelength, and frequency are related to the energy of a wave.

Investigate Music:
Demonstration shows how frequency and wavelength are related to the keys of musical notes.

Comparing Waves: Drawings show how a transverse wave and longitudinal wave are similar and different.

Performance-Based Assessment

See Unit 1, Lesson 1

2. Answers will vary. Sample answer: The light shines through the surface of the water but has no other effect on it.

4. Answers will vary. Sample answer: The tuning fork causes the surface of the water to move.

5. Answers will vary. Sample answer: The sound waves moved the surface of the water, but the light waves did not.

6. Sound waves are mechanical waves. Light waves are electromagnetic waves.

7. Answers will vary. Sample answer: In Steps 2 and 4, the water moved when the sound waves were produced. This is because mechanical waves move through a medium. They moved from the air into the water, making the water ripple. Light waves did not have this effect because they are not transmitted by vibrating particles of matter.

Unit Review
Vocabulary

1. **electromagnetic See Unit 1, Lesson 1**

2. **wavelength See Unit 1, Lesson 2**

3. **frequency See Unit 1, Lesson 2**

4. **mechanical See Unit 1, Lesson 1**

5. **amplitude See Unit 1, Lesson 2**

Key Concepts

6. A   9. B   12. A
7. B   10. D
8. D   11. C

6. **A See Unit 1, Lesson 2**

A is correct because the amplitude of sound waves corresponds to volume: the greater the amplitude, the louder the volume.

B is incorrect because the wave period is the time it takes for a full wavelength to pass a specific point and does not affect volume.

C is incorrect because wavelength is the distance from a point on one wave to a corresponding point on another wave and does not affect volume.

D is incorrect because wave speed is the speed at which a wave travels and does not affect volume.

7. **B See Unit 1, Lesson 2**

A incorrect because a diagram of a wave does not explain what a wave is.

B is correct because waves are disturbances that transfer energy.

C is incorrect because it describes absorption (in optics).

D is incorrect because "circles spreading out" is an idea to describe a wave characteristic.

8. **D See Unit 1, Lesson 2**

A is incorrect because wave period is the time required for corresponding points on consecutive waves to pass a given point.

B is incorrect because frequency is the number of waves produced in a given amount of time.

C is incorrect because amplitude is the maximum distance that the particles of a wave's medium vibrate from their rest position.

D is correct because wavelength is the distance from any point on a wave to an identical point on the next wave, such as crest to crest.

9. **B See Unit 1, Lesson 1**

A is incorrect because radio waves have the longest wavelengths, and thus the lowest frequency, in the electromagnetic spectrum.

B is correct because gamma rays have the shortest wavelengths, and thus the highest frequency, in the electromagnetic spectrum.

C is incorrect because light waves do not have the highest frequency in the electromagnetic spectrum.

D   is incorrect because x-rays do not have the highest frequency in the electromagnetic spectrum.

10. D See Unit 1, Lesson 1

A   is incorrect because light waves are not produced by earthquakes.

B   is incorrect because sound waves are not earthquake waves.

C   is incorrect because longitudinal waves move back and forth in the direction of vibration.

D   is correct because transverse waves move perpendicular to the direction of vibration, in this case, moving rock particles up and down.

11. C See Unit 1, Lesson 1

A   is incorrect because electromagnetic waves do not have to travel through a medium.

B   is incorrect because there are no gases to create an atmosphere in space.

C   is correct because electromagnetic waves cause disturbances in electric and magnetic fields.

D   is incorrect because electromagnetic waves travel at the speed of light (about 186,000 miles per second).

12. A See Unit 1, Lesson 2

A   is correct because hertz is a unit used in measurements of the number of wave cycles per second.

B   is incorrect because one wave period is the time it takes for two corresponding points on

successive waves to pass a given point.

C   is incorrect because the wave crest is the highest point on a wave.

D   is incorrect because minutes are units of time and do not describe frequency.

13. B See Unit 1, Lesson 2

A   is in incorrect because mechanical waves travel through various media at different speeds.

B   is correct because mechanical waves generally travel faster in solids than liquids, and faster in liquids than gases.

C   is in incorrect because mechanical waves generally travel faster in solids than liquids, and faster in liquids than gasses.

D   is incorrect because only mechanical waves do not travel at the speed of light.

Critical Thinking

14. See Unit 1, Lesson 2

- A loud sound wave has more energy than a quiet sound. This is because the loud sound wave has a higher amplitude and transfers more energy to the eardrum.

15. See Unit 1, Lesson 2

- The passing of a wave caused the buoy to bob up and down. When the crest of a wave passed, the buoy rose up; when a trough passed, the buoy dipped down.

- The shorter a wave period and higher the frequency, the more rapidly the buoys would bob up and down.

- The waves did not directly move the buoys or the water, because waves only move through the water.

- Waves only transfer energy, not matter such as the water itself or the buoys.

Connect Essential Questions

16. See Unit 1, Lesson 1 and Lesson 2

- The band playing set up vibrations in air that traveled to Jung as sound waves.

- The band sounded fainter to Jung and other listeners far from the stage because the energy of the sound waves decreased as they moved farther from the band. High frequency waves (singer's voice) typically lose energy more readily than low frequency waves (drums and bass).

- The energy of the sound waves decreased for two reasons. The sound waves moved through air by causing air particles to vibrate. Some energy is lost as particles rubbed against each other, creating friction that took energy from the sound waves. In addition, the waves spread out in circles called wavefronts. As the wavefronts expanded, the energy in the waves was spread out over a larger area and are therefore, reduced at any specific point on the wavefront.

Unit Test A
Key Concepts

1. B	5. D	9. A
2. D	6. C	10. D
3. B	7. A	11. D
4. C	8. D	12. A

1. B

A is incorrect because a mechanical wave slows down when it moves from a solid into a gas.

B is correct because a mechanical wave speeds up when it moves from a liquid into a solid.

C is incorrect because a mechanical wave cannot travel in a vacuum.

D is incorrect because a mechanical wave cannot travel in a vacuum.

2. D

A is incorrect because period is the time, not the distance, between two crests.

B is incorrect because frequency is a measure of how many waves pass a point in a given time.

C is incorrect because amplitude is the height of the wave, not the length.

D is correct because wavelength is the distance from one point on a wave to the corresponding point on the next wave.

3. B

A is incorrect because speed cannot be determined by time and number of peaks.

B is correct because frequency can be measured by counting the number of peaks that pass in a given amount of time.

C is incorrect because amplitude is a measure of the height of a wave.

D is incorrect because wavelength is the distance

between corresponding parts of consecutive waves.

4. C

A is incorrect because radar uses radio waves.

B is incorrect because television is transmitted in the radio region.

C is correct because visible light is between near infrared and ultraviolet light.

D is incorrect because cosmic rays are in the region of gamma rays.

5. D

A is incorrect because point 1 is closest to the source of the waves.

B is incorrect because the point of least energy is the farthest point from the source, and point 2 is not the farthest.

C is incorrect because the point of least energy is the farthest point from the source, and point 3 is not the farthest point.

D is correct because point 4 is the farthest point from the source, and energy of a wave decreases with distance as the wave spreads out and loses energy to the medium.

6. C

A is incorrect because longitudinal waves travel outward from the source and parallel to the direction of the disturbance.

B is incorrect because longitudinal waves do not move in circles.

C is correct because longitudinal waves travel parallel to the direction of the disturbance.

D is incorrect because transverse waves, not longitudinal waves, travel perpendicular to the direction of the disturbance.

7. A

A is correct because a mechanical wave travels fastest in a solid.

B is incorrect because a mechanical wave travels faster in a solid than in a liquid.

C is incorrect because a mechanical wave travels faster in a solid than in a gas.

D is incorrect because a mechanical wave travels faster in a solid than in a gas.

8. D

A is incorrect because speed equals wavelength multiplied by frequency.

B is incorrect because speed equals wavelength multiplied by frequency.

C is incorrect because speed equals wavelength multiplied by frequency.

D is correct because speed equals wavelength multiplied by frequency.

9. A

A is correct because a particle in a medium returns to about its original position.

B is incorrect because a particle in a medium returns to about its original position.

C is incorrect because a particle in a medium does not travel with a wave.

D is incorrect because a particle vibrates around its original position only while the wave is passing through.

10. D

A is incorrect because mechanical waves can move through solids.

B is incorrect because mechanical waves do not have an inherent limit to how fast they can move.

C is incorrect because the amplitude of the wave doesn't necessarily relate to its speed.

D is correct because mechanical waves must move through a medium. Depending on the medium, the speed of the wave may be affected.

11. D

A is incorrect because mechanical waves can be longitudinal waves.

B is incorrect because mechanical waves can be transverse waves.

C is incorrect because mechanical waves cannot travel through empty space.

D is correct because mechanical waves cannot travel through empty space and must travel through a medium.

12. A

A is correct because the medium is the material that is disturbed as the sound wave travels through it. The material in this example is air.

B is incorrect because the medium is not the energy transferred by the wave.

C is incorrect because sound waves cannot travel through empty space. The sound wave in this example is traveling through air.

D is incorrect because vibrations occur in the medium; they are not the medium.

Critical Thinking
13.

• description of sound waves created by tuning fork (e.g., *The tuning fork vibrates; The vibration of the tuning fork causes particles to vibrate, and they travel as a sound wave; etc.*)

• comparison of water to air (e.g., *Sound travels faster in liquids than in gases; etc.*)

Extended Response
14.

• Light waves are electromagnetic waves.

• Electromagnetic waves can travel through empty space.

• Sound waves are mechanical waves.

• Mechanical waves cannot travel through empty space.

• To observe sound or light, the waves have to reach the observer.

Unit Test B
Key Concepts

1. A	5. A	9. A
2. D	6. C	10. D
3. C	7. A	11. A
4. A	8. D	12. A

1. A

A is correct because a mechanical wave slows down when it moves from a solid into a gas.

B is incorrect because a mechanical wave speeds up when it moves from a liquid into a solid.

C is incorrect because a mechanical wave cannot travel in a vacuum.

D is incorrect because a mechanical wave cannot travel in a vacuum.

2. D

A is incorrect because period is the time, not the distance, between two crests.

B is incorrect because frequency is a measure of how many waves pass a point in a given time.

C is incorrect because amplitude is the height of the wave, not the length.

D is correct because wavelength is the distance from one point on a wave to the corresponding point on the next wave.

3. C

A is incorrect because amplitude is a measure of the intensity of the sound wave.

B is incorrect because speed cannot be determined by the time between sound waves alone.

C is correct because frequency can be measured by the inverse of the time between sound waves.

D   is incorrect because
wavelength is the distance
between corresponding
compressions in the sound
wave.

4. A

A   is correct because
electromagnetic waves
consist of vibrating electric
and magnetic fields.

B   is incorrect because it
describes a longitudinal
wave, and electromagnetic
waves are transverse waves.

C   is incorrect because
electromagnetic waves all
travel at the same speed in a
vacuum.

D   is incorrect because
electromagnetic waves all
travel at the same speed in a
vacuum.

5. A

A   is correct because point 1 is
closest to the source of the
waves.

B   is incorrect because the point
of most energy is the closest
point from the source, and
point 2 is not the closest.

C   is incorrect because the point
of most energy is the closest
point from the source, and
point 3 is not the closest.

D   is incorrect because point 4 is
the farthest point from the
source, and energy of a wave
decreases with distance as the
wave spreads out and loses
energy to the medium.

6. C

A   is incorrect because a
longitudinal waves travel
outward from the source of

the source and parallel to the
direction of the disturbance.

B   is incorrect because
longitudinal waves do not
move in circles.

C   is correct because
longitudinal waves travel
parallel to the direction of the
disturbance.

D   is incorrect because
transverse waves, not
longitudinal waves, travel
perpendicular to the direction
of the disturbance.

7. A

A   is correct because a
mechanical wave travels
faster through hot air. The
particles in hot air move
faster than the particles in
cold air.

B   is incorrect because a
mechanical wave travels
faster through hot air. The
particles in hot air move
faster than the particles in
cold air.

C   is incorrect because a
mechanical wave travels
slower in a denser medium. A
liquid is more dense than hot
or cold air.

D   is incorrect because a
mechanical wave travels
slower in a denser medium. A
solid is more dense than a
liquid or hot or cold air.

8. D

A   is incorrect because speed is
equal to wavelength
multiplied by frequency.

B   is incorrect because speed is
equal to wavelength
multiplied by frequency.

C   is incorrect because speed is
equal to wavelength
multiplied by frequency.

D   is correct because speed is
equal to wavelength
multiplied by frequency.

9. A

A   is correct because a particle
in a medium returns to about
its original position.

B   is incorrect because a particle
vibrates around its original
position only while the wave
is passing through.

C   is incorrect because a particle
in a medium does not travel
with a wave.

D   is incorrect because a particle
in a medium returns to about
its original position.

10. D

A   is incorrect because wave II
travels much slower than the
other waves, but
electromagnetic waves travel
in air and water close to the
speed of light, which is the
fastest speed possible.

B   is incorrect because
electromagnetic waves all
travel close to the speed of
light in air and water, but
wave II is traveling much
slower than the speed of light.

C   is incorrect because wave II
travels much slower than the
speed of light, but
electromagnetic waves travel
close to the speed of light in
air and water.

D   is correct because waves I
and III both travel close to
the speed of light in air and
water.

11. A

A is correct because mechanical waves cannot travel through empty space and must travel through a medium.

B is incorrect because mechanical waves can be longitudinal waves.

C is incorrect because mechanical waves can be transverse waves.

D is incorrect because mechanical waves cannot travel through empty space.

12. A

A is correct because the medium is the material that is disturbed as the sound wave travels through it. The material in this example is air.

B is incorrect because the medium is not the energy transferred by the wave.

C is incorrect because sound waves cannot travel through empty space. The sound wave in this example is traveling through air.

D is incorrect because vibrations occur in the medium; they are not the medium.

Critical Thinking
13.

- Andrew's partner

- explanation of why Andrew's partner hears the sound first (e.g., *Sound waves travel faster in water than they do in air; etc.*)

Extended Response
14.

- A mechanical wave causes water particles to move back and forth.

- An electromagnetic wave involves vibrations in electric and magnetic fields.

- Both types of waves transfer energy.

Unit 2 Sound
Unit Pretest

1. A	5. B	9. C
2. B	6. B	10. A
3. C	7. D	
4. C	8. D	

1. A

A is correct because mechanical waves move more quickly through a solid than through a gas.

B is incorrect because mechanical waves move more slowly in a gas than they do in a solid.

C is incorrect because mechanical waves change speed when they change media.

D is incorrect because the speed of mechanical waves remains the same in any particular medium.

2. B

A is incorrect because the pits store electronic data, not sound waves.

B is correct because the pits store data that can be read by a laser and digitally translated into sound.

C is incorrect because the pits are not created by sound waves.

D is incorrect because the pits store data that can be translated into sound.

3. C

A is incorrect because sound isn't perceived differently whether it is in front or behind of you.

B is incorrect because the Doppler effect states that increasing distance means decreased frequency or pitch.

C is correct because decreasing pitch occurs when a sound's source is moving away.

D is incorrect because a change in the pitch of the sound indicates a change in distance between you and the sound source.

4. C

A is incorrect because a wave's amplitude or intensity doesn't depend on frequency.

B is incorrect because a wave's amplitude or intensity doesn't depend on frequency.

C is correct because decreasing frequency means increasing wavelength.

D is incorrect because decreasing the frequency will increase the wavelength.

5. B

A is incorrect because sound waves are a type of longitudinal wave.

B is correct because sound waves are a type of longitudinal wave.

C is incorrect because sound waves are a type of longitudinal wave.

D is incorrect because sound waves are a type of longitudinal wave.

6. B

A   is incorrect because the sound wave would travel faster in a hotter climate.

B   is correct because the speed of sound increases when the temperature of the media increases.

C   is incorrect because sound waves travel slower in cold areas.

D   is incorrect because sound requires a medium to propagate.

7. D

A   is incorrect because a light wave is a type of electromagnetic wave.

B   is incorrect because a water wave is a type of transverse mechanical wave.

C   is incorrect because a transverse wave does not have compressions.

D   is correct because longitudinal waves contain compressions and rarefactions.

8. D

A   is incorrect because constructive interference combines two waves into one larger wave.

B   is incorrect because destructive interference cancels out two waves.

C   is incorrect because absorption would result in a much smaller secondary set of waves.

D   is correct because the reflection of the sound produces a secondary set of waves.

9. C

A   is incorrect because a sonic boom relates to the speed of an object, not its altitude.

B   is incorrect because the sound is significantly louder than a backfire of any engine.

C   is correct because sonic booms are due to sound waves produced from objects traveling faster than the speed of sound.

D   is incorrect because reflected waves have the same or less intensity as their original waves.

10. A

A   is correct because during an ultrasound procedure, ultrasonic waves are sent into a patient's body; these sound waves reflect off internal organs, then are detected by a device that changes the reflected waves into an image.

B   is incorrect because during an ultrasound procedure, ultrasonic waves, not ultraviolet waves, are sent into a patient's body.

C   is incorrect because during an ultrasound procedure, ultrasonic waves reflect off the patient's internal organs to produce an image.

D   is incorrect because during an ultrasound procedure, ultrasonic waves, not ultraviolet waves, reflect off the patient's internal organs to produce an image.

Lesson 1 Quiz

1. A   4. B
2. D   5. D
3. C

1. A

A   is correct because pitch decreases with increasing wavelength.

B   is incorrect because loudness is not affected by wavelength.

C   is incorrect because amplitude is not affected by wavelength.

D   is incorrect because frequency decreases with increasing wavelength.

2. D

A   is incorrect because heat might burn the person, but would not burn the eardrum.

B   is incorrect because there are no explosive materials inside the ear.

C   is incorrect because sound waves are longitudinal, or compression, waves.

D   is correct because sound waves are compression waves and can cause vibration too large for the eardrum to sustain.

3. C

A   is incorrect because a wave can move in any direction and "side to side" is unclear.

B   is incorrect because a wave can move in any direction and "up and down" is unclear.

C   is correct because sound waves are longitudinal

waves, which move parallel to the direction of the wave.

D   is incorrect because sound waves are longitudinal waves, which move parallel to the direction of the wave.

4. B

A   is incorrect because the inner ear cannot block unwanted sounds.

B   is correct because vibrations in the inner ear are converted to electrical signals, which are then interpreted by the brain.

C   is incorrect because sounds from different locations do not affect the inner ear differently.

D   is incorrect because the inner ear does not reflect frequencies.

5. D

A   is incorrect because the speed of the wave does not change.

B   is incorrect because the medium stays constant during a Doppler effect.

C   is incorrect because the Doppler effect relates to frequency not amplitude.

D   is correct because a change in frequency of a sound wave is involved in the Doppler effect.

Lesson 2 Quiz
1. B   4. A
2. B   5. A
3. A

1. B

A   is incorrect because interference is a phenomenon occurring between two waves.

B   is correct because the sound wave matches the vibrational frequency of the windows.

C   is incorrect because sound waves may be reflected but the reflections do not cause the window to vibrate.

D   is incorrect because an echo is a type of reflection, and reflections do not cause windows to vibrate.

2. B

A   is incorrect because sound waves travel faster when the temperature of the medium increases.

B   is correct because sound travels faster when the temperature of the medium is higher.

C   is incorrect because the speed of sound will increase when either gas or liquid is heated.

D   is incorrect because the speed of sound will increase when either gas or liquid is heated.

3. A

A   is correct because many reflections create echoes, which redirect sounds.

B   is incorrect because the air outside is not always colder than inside.

C   is incorrect because constructive interference from walls and wood floors is not common.

D   is incorrect because vibrations in windows affect sounds inside and outside equally.

4. A

A   is correct because hard, smooth surfaces reflect sound waves best.

B   is incorrect because irregular surfaces cause random reflections of sound waves.

C   is incorrect because soft surfaces dampen the amplitude of sound waves.

D   is incorrect because irregular water surfaces scatter sound waves.

5. A

A   is correct because constructive interference involves two or more waves combining to increase wave amplitude.

B   is incorrect because destructive interference would cause the sounds to cancel.

C   is incorrect because the air temperature difference would not be significant enough to increase the loudness relative to other locations.

D   is incorrect because resonance involves the vibration from sounds.

Lesson 3 Quiz
1. D   4. A
2. B   5. B
3. B

1. D

A   is incorrect because sonar is not used to create images of internal body structures.

B   is incorrect because radar is not used to create images of internal body structures.

C is incorrect because it is ultrasound technology that uses high-frequency sound waves to produce images of internal body structures.

D is correct because ultrasound technology uses high-frequency sound waves to produce images of internal body structures.

2. B

A is incorrect because echolocation does not involve the use of light waves.

B is correct because echolocation refers to the use of reflected sound waves to locate objects.

C is incorrect because echolocation does not involve the use of any light waves, including ultraviolet waves.

D is incorrect because echolocation does not involve the use of only ultrasonic waves, but of sound waves of many frequencies.

3. B

A is incorrect because the speaker changes electrical signals into sound waves.

B is correct because the microphone changes sound waves into electrical signals.

C is incorrect because only the microphone changes sound waves into electrical signals.

D is incorrect because the speaker changes electrical signals into sound waves and the microphone changes sound waves into electrical signals.

4. A

A is correct because sonar is often used to locate underwater objects such as shipwrecks.

B is incorrect because laser technology, not sonar, is used in microscopic surgery.

C is incorrect because sonar is used to locate objects on Earth, not in space.

D is incorrect because it is ultrasound technology, not sonar, that is used to create images of internal organs.

5. B

A is incorrect because the depth does not affect the amount of data that can be stored.

B is correct because decreasing the width between tracks would allow more data to be encoded.

C is incorrect because if the pits overlapped, data would not be clearly organized.

D is incorrect because the wavelength of the laser does not affect what is encoded on the CD.

Lesson 1 Alternative Assessment

Make a Two- or Three-Dimensional Model: Models should be accurate, comprehensive, and neat. The model should include all necessary labels. The important concepts related to the model should be clear.

Make a Digital Presentation: Presentations should be organized and clear and correctly describe the characteristics of sound waves.

Gather Data and Make a Bar Graph: Graphs should be organized, neat, and accurate. Graphs should include 10 different sounds.

Write a Story: The story should include a description of a sound wave and should describe the parts of the ear.

Make a Crossword Puzzle: The clues used for the puzzle should show an understanding of the terms used. An answer key is included.

Write and Perform a Puppet Show: The skit should include an accurate description of how and why hearing damage occurs and should explain how to prevent hearing damage.

Lesson 2 Alternative Assessment

I Can't Hear You! Oral presentation clearly explains how constructive interference and destructive interference are both possible.

Echo, Echo, Echo: Sketch indicates stage and hall walls; arrows correctly indicate the movement of sound waves.

Stay Out! Plan should include how exterior sounds will be kept out and what materials will be used.

What a Pit! Orchestra pit sketch indicates how instrument sounds interact.

Too Much Noise! Presentation lists several sound-absorbing methods.

Constructive Criticism:
Model shows where the musicians sit in relation to audience members.

A Resounding Success:
Demonstration clearly explains resonance and tells how it can be increased or decreased.

Tuning Up: Instructions clearly explain how to use a tuning fork to tune a piano.

Standing Wave: Diagram shows the standing wave and air movement made by a wind instrument and explains why the sounds become louder.

Lesson 3 Alternative Assessment

Top Row: Students should identify devices that use sound technology they use every day and briefly describe how they work. Devices may include cell phones, MP3 players, landlines, etc.

Middle Row: Students should identify a specific effort (such as the *Titantic* exploration) and explain how sonar made it possible.

Students should identify a speech from history that is meaningful to us today. Student should consider speeches from Martin Luther King, Jr., Winston Churchill, or other historical figures who are relevant to the study of history or to life today.

Bottom Row: Students should verbalize how the process works: To store sound on a computer file, the sound is changed into electrical signals and then stored as a digital file on the computer

hard drive. Speakers change the signal back to sound.

Students should explain how various animals use echolocation, including how they "sense" or hear echoes. Animals may include bats, dolphins, toothed whales, shrews, and oilbirds.

Students should explain in detail how tumors and fetuses can be identified via ultrasound, as well as how medical problems can be averted.

Performance-Based Assessment

See Unit 2, Lesson 1

1. Answers will vary, but students should note that one tuning fork is smaller in size than the other. Students should also record the frequency values stamped into each tuning fork.

2. Answers will vary. Students may correctly predict that the smaller tuning fork with the higher frequency will have a higher pitch.

5. Answers will vary. Sample answer: The tuning fork made a faint sound when held in the air. It made a louder sound when it was touching the solid object.

6. Answers will vary. Sample answer: The tuning fork made a faint sound when held in the air. It made a louder sound when it was touching the solid object.

7. The larger fork is marked with a lower frequency. The smaller fork is marked with a higher frequency.

8. Answers will vary. Sample answer: The smaller tuning fork with the higher frequency had a higher pitch.

9. The higher the frequency, the higher the pitch of sound it makes.

10. Answers will vary. Sample answer: The sound was more noticeable when the sound waves traveled into the solid object because the particles in a solid are closer together than particles of a gas.

Unit Review
Vocabulary
1. **T See Unit 2, Lesson 1**
2. **F See Unit 2, Lesson 1**
3. **F See Unit 2, Lesson 2**
4. **T See Unit 2, Lesson 2**
5. **T See Unit 2, Lesson 3**

Key Concepts
6. B	9. A	12. C
7. D	10. A	13. B
8. C	11. B	

6. B See Unit 2, Lesson 1

A is incorrect because the amplitude of a sound wave does not describe how humans hear the sound.

B is correct because parts inside the ear covert the sound wayes to electrical signals, which are sent to the brain.

C is incorrect because electrical signals, not sound waves, go to the brain.

D is incorrect because the eardrum does not convert sound waves to sound, but passes along the vibrations to other parts of the ear.

7. D See Unit 2, Lesson 2

A   is incorrect because destructive interference involves overlapping sound waves that reduce amplitude and does not explain why the guitar string vibrated in response to the tuning fork.

B   is incorrect because ultrasonic frequencies and human hearing have nothing to do with why the tuning fork caused the guitar string to vibrate.

C   is incorrect because identifying sound waves as mechanical waves does not explain why the string vibrated without being touched.

D   is correct because resonance results when two objects have the same natural frequency of vibration.

8. C See Unit 2, Lesson 1

A   is incorrect because sound waves do not create tensions and accumulations as they move through a medium.

B   is incorrect because an echo is created by reflected sound waves and does not describe the changes in the medium.

C   is correct because sound waves are longitudinal waves that cause compressions and rarefactions in the medium.

D   is incorrect because a sound wave is a mechanical wave, and one does not create the other.

9. A See Unit 2, Lesson 2

A   is correct because heavy curtains are soft materials

that partially absorb sound waves.

B   is incorrect because hardwood floors are hard surfaces and reflect sound waves.

C   is incorrect because brick walls are hard surfaces and reflect sound waves.

D   is incorrect because cement floors are hard surfaces and reflect sound waves.

10. A See Unit 2, Lesson 1

A   is correct because G points to a wave crest, and F is wavelength because it measures the distance between two wave crests.

B   is incorrect because E does not represent a wavelength.

C   is incorrect because H does not point to a crest and E does not represent a wavelength.

D   is incorrect because H does not point to a crest.

11. B See Unit 2, Lesson 3

A   is incorrect because bats send out ultrasonic waves that echo back after striking objects.

B   is correct because sending messages over telephone lines has nothing to do with echolocation.

C   is incorrect because dolphins use reflected sound waves to locate fish.

D   is incorrect because ocean floor mapping uses sound waves that are reflected from the ocean floor and bounce back to a receiver.

12. C See Unit 2, Lesson 1

A   is incorrect because thunder does not always take 15 seconds to travel.

B   is incorrect because the sound waves of thunder moved through air and light waves do not have to move through any medium.

C   is correct because the flash of lighting was conveyed by electromagnetic waves moving at the speed of light, but the thunder was conveyed by mechanical sound waves moving much more slowly through the medium of air.

D   is incorrect because electromagnetic light waves always travel at the same speed and do not need to move through a medium.

13. B See Unit 2, Lesson 2

A   is incorrect because sound waves travel faster through closely packed media than loosely packed media.

B   is correct because the closer the particles in a medium are, the more readily that they transfer the sound wave.

C   is incorrect because sound waves travel more slowly through a loosely packed medium than a closely packed medium.

D   is incorrect because sound waves can travel through media that are made up of particles.

Critical Thinking

14. See Unit 2, Lesson 1

• identifies the cochlea is part of the human ear (e.g., *The* cochlea is located in the inner ear; humans have two cochlea, one in each ear.)

- identifies the parts of the cochlea (e.g., *The cochlea contains liquid, hair cells, and nerve cells.*)

- demonstrates understanding of how sound waves are changed into electrical signals and sent to the brain (e.g., *Vibrations in the inner ear create waves in the liquid, which bend the hair cells and stimulate nerve cells to send electrical signals to the brain.*)

15. See Unit 2, Lesson 1

- recognizes that sounds have pitch and pitch can change when frequency changes (e.g., *The sound of the train whistle grows to a higher pitch as the train comes closer then drops to a lower pitch as the train moves away.*)

- identifies the Doppler Effect as an observed change in the frequency of a sound wave (e.g., *The change in pitch comes from the Doppler Effect. The actual frequency does not change. It just seems to the people on the platform that it changes.*)

- demonstrates understanding that shorter wavelengths and higher frequencies create higher pitched sounds. (e.g., *As the space between the train and people on the platform decreases, the wavelengths grow shorter and the frequencies higher.*)

- demonstrates understanding that longer wavelengths and

lower frequencies create lower pitched sounds. (e.g., *As the distance between the train and people on the platform increases, the sound waves spread out, creating longer wavelengths and lower frequencies.*)

Connect Essential Questions

16. See Unit 2, Lesson 1 and Lesson 2

- demonstrates understanding of interference (e.g., *The sound barrier is caused by wave interference. As the jet speeds up, sound waves in front of the jet plane get closer together and finally overlap. They combine by constructive interference, which increases the amplitude of the sound waves. The constructive interference results in the sound barrier.*)

- identifies how sound waves travel through a medium (e.g., *Vibrations from the jet engines create sound waves in the air around the plane. A jet breaks the sound barrier by flying faster than the speed of its own sound waves.*)

- demonstrates understanding that the speed of sound depends upon the medium and its temperature (e.g., *It is possible for a jet at high altitude to fly faster than the speed of sound, be-cause the speed of sound in air is lower in the cold temperatures at high altitudes.*)

- demonstrates understanding of how human ears hear sound.

(e.g., *Breaking the sound barrier creates a shock wave. When the shock wave enters the ear, you hear it as an explosive sonic boom.*)

Unit Test A
Key Concepts

1. D	5. C	9. C
2. C	6. B	10. C
3. C	7. A	11. B
4. C	8. C	12. C

1. D

A is incorrect because the height of the hill doesn't change with the seasons.

B is incorrect because the frequency of their voices would remain constant.

C is incorrect because air pressure has little effect on the speed of sound.

D is correct because the air temperature is colder in winter than during the summer, which causes sound to travel slower.

2. C

A is incorrect because a crest is the maximum point of a transverse wave.

B is incorrect because a trough is the minimum point of a transverse wave.

C is correct because the rarefactions are the area of the longitudinal wave with the lowest density of particles.

D is incorrect because compressions are the area of the longitudinal wave with the highest density of particles.

3. C

A is incorrect because a bat's use of ultrasonic waves is an example of echolocation, not resonance.

B is incorrect because resonance happens when a sound wave matches the natural frequency of an object, causing the object to vibrate.

C is correct because resonance happens when a sound wave matches the natural frequency of an object, causing the object to vibrate.

D is incorrect because sonic booms result from constructive interference, not resonance.

4. C

A is incorrect because the outer ear is responsible for capturing sound waves.

B is incorrect because the middle ear transmits the energy of the sound wave from the air to cochlear fluid.

C is correct because the inner ear converts sound waves into electrical signals.

D is incorrect because the ear does not filter out sound waves.

5. C

A is incorrect because both CDs and digital files are devices on which people store sounds.

B is incorrect because both audio CDs and digital files store information digitally, which requires the use of a computer.

C is correct because an audio CD stores sounds as pits on the CD's surface, whereas a digital CD stores sounds as computer code.

D is incorrect because the information stored on both devices can be converted into sound waves.

6. B

A is incorrect because the greater the amplitude of a sound wave, the louder the sound; therefore, a string with a smaller vibration would produce a softer sound.

B is correct because the greater the amplitude of a sound wave, the louder the sound; therefore, a string with a greater vibration would produce a louder sound.

C is incorrect because a longer string would produce a lower-pitched sound; loudness depends on the amplitude of a sound wave.

D is incorrect because a shorter string would produce a higher-pitched sound; loudness depends on the amplitude of a sound wave.

7. A

A is correct because the two vehicles are moving at the same speed; therefore, the vehicles are not moving relative to each other, and there is no Doppler effect.

B is incorrect because the two vehicles are moving at the same speed; therefore, the vehicles are not moving

relative to each other, and there is no Doppler effect.

C is incorrect because the two vehicles are moving at the same speed; therefore, the vehicles are not moving relative to each other, and there is no Doppler effect.

D is incorrect because the two vehicles are moving at the same speed; therefore, the vehicles are not moving relative to each other, and there is no Doppler effect.

8. C

A is incorrect because sonar is a technology developed primarily for underwater detection.

B is incorrect because ultrasound technology is a medical technique.

C is correct because bats produce ultrasonic waves for echolocation.

D is incorrect because Doppler effects relate to frequency changes of sounds.

9. C

A is incorrect because the switch connects the telephone to the transmitting phone lines.

B is incorrect because the wall jack is the port in the wall into which the phone cord plugs.

C is correct because the microphone is the part that is spoken into that produces electrical signals.

D is incorrect because the speaker produces the sound in the earpiece.

10. C

A is incorrect because sounds travel fastest through solids, slower in liquids, and still slower in gases.

B is incorrect because sounds travel fastest through solids, slower in liquids, and still slower in gases.

C is correct because sounds travel fastest through solids, slower in liquids, and still slower in gases.

D is incorrect because sounds travel fastest through solids, slower in liquids, and still slower in gases.

11. B

A is incorrect because smooth, hard surfaces reflect sound waves well.

B is correct because foam will absorb sound and minimize echoing.

C is incorrect because smooth, hard surfaces reflect sound waves well.

D is incorrect because smooth, hard surfaces reflect sound waves well.

12. C

A is incorrect because this diagram shows the constructive interference of two transverse waves.

B is incorrect because this diagram shows the constructive interference of two longitudinal waves.

C is correct because this diagram shows the destructive interference of two transverse waves.

D is incorrect because this diagram shows the destructive interference of two longitudinal waves.

Critical Thinking
13.

• sound rate increases with increasing temperature

• an explanation for sound speed based on particle density (e.g., *Higher temperatures mean higher kinetic energies; Particles that are moving around faster have more collisions, and therefore the sound wave propagates through the medium faster*; etc.)

Extended Response
14.

• explanation of why alarm A has the highest pitch (e.g., *The pitch of a sound depends on the frequency of the sound wave. Higher frequency waves have higher pitches. In a given medium, as the wavelength of a sound wave decreases, its frequency increases. Because alarm A has the shortest wavelength, it has the highest frequency, and therefore it has the highest pitch*; etc.)

• alarm A

• explanation of why alarm A is loudest (e.g., *The loudness of a sound is measured in decibels. Alarm A has the highest decibel level, so it is the loudest alarm*; etc.)

Unit Test B
Key Concepts

1.	B	5.	D	9.	C
2.	D	6.	A	10.	B
3.	A	7.	B	11.	B
4.	A	8.	B	12.	A

1. B

A is incorrect because wavelength and frequency would not change from one time of the year to another.

B is correct because the air temperature is colder in winter than during the summer, which causes sound to travel slower.

C is incorrect because the concert was performed outside and therefore the medium was the air.

D is incorrect because the density of the particles in the air would not vary significantly because air is a gas.

2. D

A is incorrect because the wave does not change the size of the particles.

B is incorrect because a wave transports energy but not the medium.

C is incorrect because a wave transports energy but not the medium.

D is correct because the particles are pushed into a compression and then pulled into another rarefaction.

3. A

A is correct because resonance happens when a sound wave matches the natural frequency of an object, causing the object to vibrate.

B   is incorrect because the reflecting sound waves are examples of echoes, not resonance.

C   is incorrect because resonance happens when a sound wave matches the natural frequency of an object, causing the object to vibrate.

D   is incorrect because the alternating pattern of loud and soft sounds is an example of a beat, not resonance.

4. **A**

A   is correct because the outer ear is responsible for capturing sound waves.

B   is incorrect because the middle ear transmits the energy of the sound wave from the air to cochlear fluid.

C   is incorrect because the inner ear converts sound waves into electrical signals.

D   is incorrect because the ear does not filter out sound waves.

5. **D**

A   is incorrect because although CDs and digital files both preserve sounds in the form of stored information, the sound waves themselves do not exist for years.

B   is incorrect because all sound waves lose energy over time.

C   is incorrect because an audio CD stores sounds in the form of pits along the CD's surface.

D   is correct because both audio CDs and digital files store information that can be converted into sound waves.

6. **A**

A   is correct because the greater the amplitude of a sound wave, the louder the sound; therefore, a string with a smaller vibration would produce a softer sound.

B   is incorrect because the greater the amplitude of a sound wave, the louder the sound; therefore, a string with a greater vibration would produce a louder sound.

C   is incorrect because a longer string would produce a lower-pitched sound; loudness depends on the amplitude of a sound wave.

D   is incorrect because a shorter string would produce a higher-pitched sound; loudness depends on the amplitude of a sound wave.

7. **B**

A   is incorrect because the vehicles are traveling at different speeds, so there is a Doppler effect.

B   is correct because the distance between the two cars is increasing, so the frequency will sound lower to the police officer in the second car, per the Doppler effect.

C   is incorrect because the distance between the two vehicles is increasing, not decreasing, so the frequency will sound lower to the police

officer in the second car, per the Doppler effect.

D   is incorrect because the distance between the two cars is increasing, so the frequency will sound lower to the police officer in the second car, per the Doppler effect.

8. **B**

A   is incorrect because infrared waves are electromagnetic waves. They are not used for echolocation.

B   is correct because bats produce ultrasonic waves for echolocation.

C   is incorrect because sound waves are longitudinal, not transverse, waves.

D   is incorrect because sound waves are not electromagnetic waves.

9. **C**

A   is incorrect because the mouthpiece contains a microphone that converts the incoming electrical signals into sound waves.

B   is incorrect because the mouthpiece contains a microphone that converts the incoming electrical signals into sound waves.

C   is correct because the mouthpiece contains a microphone that converts the incoming electrical signals into sound waves.

D   is incorrect because the mouthpiece contains a microphone that converts the incoming electrical signals into sound waves.

10. B

A is incorrect because sounds travel fastest through solids, slower in liquids, and still slower in gases.

B is correct because sounds travel fastest through solids, slower in liquids, and still slower in gases.

C is incorrect because sounds travel fastest through solids, slower in liquids, and still slower in gases.

D is incorrect because sounds travel fastest through solids, slower in liquids, and still slower in gases.

11. B

A is incorrect because smooth, hard surfaces reflect sound waves well.

B is correct because foam will absorb sound and minimize echoing.

C is incorrect because smooth, hard surfaces reflect sound waves well.

D is incorrect because smooth, hard surfaces reflect sound waves well.

12. A

A is correct because this diagram shows the constructive interference of two transverse waves.

B is incorrect because this diagram shows the constructive interference of two longitudinal waves.

C is incorrect because this diagram shows the destructive interference of two transverse waves.

D is incorrect because this diagram shows the destructive interference of two longitudinal waves.

Critical Thinking
13.

- sound speed is highest in solids and lowest in gases

- an explanation for sound speed based on particle density (e.g., *Sarah will discover that sound travels fastest through ice and slowest through water vapor. The reason for this is that the particle density is higher in solids, so collisions occur more frequently allowing for waves to propagate rapidly*; etc.)

Critical Thinking
14.

- alarm C

- explanation of why alarm C has the lowest pitch (e.g., *The pitch of a sound depends on the frequency of the sound wave. Lower frequency waves have lower pitches. In a given medium, as the wavelength of a sound wave increases, its frequency decreases. Because alarm C has the longest wavelength, it has the lowest frequency, and therefore it has the lowest pitch*; etc.)

- alarm A

- explanation of why alarm A produces a sound wave with the greatest amplitude (e.g., *The loudness of a sound is measured in decibels. Alarm A has the highest decibel level,*

so it is the loudest alarm. The greater the amplitude of a sound wave, the louder the sound. Because alarm A is the loudest alarm, it produces sound waves that have the greatest amplitude; etc.)

Unit 3 Light
Unit Pretest

1. D	5. D	9. C
2. C	6. C	10. C
3. A	7. A	
4. C	8. A	

1. D

A is incorrect because ultraviolet waves, not microwaves, have more energy (higher frequency, shorter wavelength) than visible light waves.

B is incorrect because ultraviolet waves, not radio waves, have more energy (higher frequency, shorter wavelength) than visible light waves.

C is incorrect because ultraviolet waves, not infrared waves, have more energy (higher frequency, shorter wavelength) than visible light waves.

D is correct because ultraviolet waves have more energy (higher frequency, shorter wavelength) than visible light waves.

2. C

A is incorrect because an electromagnetic wave with a long wavelength has a low frequency.

B is incorrect because an electromagnetic wave with a

long wavelength has a low frequency and low energy.

C is correct because an electromagnetic wave with a long wavelength has a low frequency and can travel through a vacuum.

D is incorrect because an electromagnetic wave does not require a medium to travel through. These waves can travel through a vacuum.

3. A

A is correct because a flat mirror will reflect light at the same angle that the light hits the mirror. The angle is measured from the imaginary line (the normal) that is perpendicular to the mirror at the point where the ray of light hits the mirror.

B is incorrect because the diagram shows a flat mirror. Convex mirrors are curved outward. Convex mirrors are also called diverging mirrors.

C is incorrect because a diverging mirror is curved outward.

D is incorrect because a convex mirror is curved inward. The diagram shows a flat mirror without a curve.

4. C

A is incorrect because beam 1 is transmitted, not scattered, by the material.

B is incorrect because beam 2 is absorbed, not scattered, by the material.

C is correct because beam 3 is scattered by the material. It spreads out in all directions.

D is incorrect because beam 4 is reflected, not scattered, by the material.

5. D

A is incorrect because blinking is an involuntary action.

B is incorrect because the eye, by way of the optic nerve, sends electric impulses to the brain. The brain then translates these impulses into images we recognize.

C is incorrect because the brain is very important to vision.

D is correct because the brain takes signals from the eyes and interprets them to provide us with information about size, shape, color, and location.

6. C

A is incorrect because the characteristic of losing very little light during transmission is not a feature of LED lights, but of fiber optics.

B is incorrect because the characteristic of losing very little light during transmission is not a feature of lasers, but of fiber optics.

C is correct because fiber optics lose very little light as they transmit and carry light.

D is incorrect because the characteristic of losing very little light during transmission is not a feature of incandescent lights, but of fiber optics.

7. A

A is correct because different colors result from light waves of different frequencies.

B is incorrect because electric currents are used to energize gases inside lightbulbs to produce electromagnetic radiation.

C is incorrect because lens change light in order to magnify images, not to produce color images.

D is incorrect because concentrating light into a very small range of wavelength produces a laser.

8. A

A is correct because label A points to the pupil. The pupil works in conjunction with the iris to change shape under varying light conditions. The change in shape allows more or less light to enter the eye, depending on the light levels.

B is incorrect because label B points to the cornea. The cornea helps refract light.

C is incorrect because label C points to the lens. The lens is responsible for focusing light images onto the retina.

D is incorrect because label D points to the retina. The retina is where light images are received from the lens before being transmitted to the brain.

9. C

A is incorrect because the combination of colors produces white light. All the light will reflect off a white surface and appear white, not black.

B is incorrect because the combination of colors

produces white light. All the light will reflect off a white surface and appear white, not orange.

C is correct because red, blue, and green are the primary colors of light. A combination of these colors produces white light. All the colors will reflect off the surface and appear white.

D is incorrect because the combination of colors produces white light. All the light will reflect off a white surface and appear white, not yellow.

10. C

A is incorrect because diverging mirrors are convex and diverging lenses are concave.

B is incorrect because diverging mirrors are convex and diverging lenses are concave.

C is correct because diverging mirrors are convex (bending outward), and diverging lenses are concave (bending inward). The difference is due to the fact that mirrors reflect light, whereas lenses refocus the light.

D is incorrect because diverging mirrors are convex and diverging lenses are concave.

Lesson 1 Quiz

1. D   4. C
2. A   5. B
3. C

1. D

A is incorrect because ultraviolet rays have more energy than infrared rays do.

B is incorrect because ultraviolet rays have a higher frequency than infrared rays do.

C is incorrect because ultraviolet rays have a shorter wavelength than infrared rays do.

D is correct because ultraviolet and infrared rays travel at the same speed, the speed of light, in a vacuum.

2. A

A is correct because all radio waves are included in the electromagnetic spectrum.

B is incorrect because sound waves are not electromagnetic waves. Radio waves are electromagnetic.

C is incorrect because ocean waves are not electromagnetic waves. Radio waves are electromagnetic.

D is incorrect because gravitational pull is not an electromagnetic wave. Radio waves are electromagnetic.

3. C

A is incorrect because wavelength is the distance between two wave crests; this is represented by label C, not A.

B is incorrect because wavelength is the distance between two wave crests; this is represented by label C, not B.

C is correct because wavelength is the distance between two wave crests; this is represented by label C.

D is incorrect because wavelength is the distance between two wave crests; this is represented by label C, not D.

4. C

A is incorrect because violet, not red, light has the shortest wavelength (highest frequency).

B is incorrect because violet, not green, light has the shortest wavelength (highest frequency).

C is correct because violet light has the shortest wavelength (highest frequency).

D is incorrect because violet, not yellow, light has the shortest wavelength (highest frequency).

5. B

A is incorrect because all electromagnetic waves travel at the same speed, which is the speed of light.

B is correct because the higher the frequency, the higher the energy. If delta rays have a higher frequency than gamma rays have, then delta rays would have more energy.

C is incorrect because if delta rays have a higher frequency than gamma rays have, then delta waves would have a shorter wavelength.

D is incorrect because if delta rays have a higher frequency than gamma rays have, then delta waves would have a shorter, not longer, wavelength.

Lesson 2 Quiz

1. C 4. D
2. B 5. A
3. C

1. C

A is incorrect because pure water is transparent and does not scatter much of the light that strikes it.

B is incorrect because a shiny mirror reflects, not scatters, most of the light that strikes it.

C is correct because frosted glass is translucent. Much of the light that travels through a translucent material is scattered, so it produces a blurry image.

D is incorrect because an eyeglass lens transmits, not scatters, most of the light that strikes it.

2. B

A is incorrect because beam 1 is transmitted, not absorbed, by the material.

B is correct because beam 2 is absorbed by the material. It stops in the material and is not transmitted, scattered, or reflected.

C is incorrect because beam 3 is scattered, not absorbed, by the material.

D is incorrect because beam 4 is reflected, not absorbed, by the material.

3. C

A is incorrect because a red rose reflects only red light. If blue light strikes the rose, the blue light will be absorbed.

As a result, the red rose will appear black.

B is incorrect because white objects reflect all light. The red rose absorbs blue light and reflects only red light.

C is correct because the red rose absorbs all colors of light except red. When blue light shines on it, the rose absorbs the light and does not reflect any light. An object that does not reflect any light appears black.

D is incorrect because the red rose absorbs all colors of light except red. If blue light shines on it, the red rose will not reflect any light.

4. D

A is incorrect because light would speed up while going from a solid to a gas.

B is incorrect because light would speed up while going from a solid to a liquid.

C is incorrect because light would speed up while going from a solid to a gas.

D is correct because light slows down while going from a vacuum to any type of matter.

5. A

A is correct because light with the shortest wavelength refracts the most. Of the four colors listed, blue light has the shortest wavelength.

B is incorrect because light with the shortest wavelength refracts the most. Green light has a longer wavelength than blue light does.

C is incorrect because light with the shortest wavelength refracts the most. Orange light has a longer wavelength than blue light does.

D is incorrect because light with the shortest wavelength refracts the most. Red light has a longer wavelength than blue light does.

Lesson 3 Quiz

1. C 4. C
2. D 5. B
3. B

1. C

A is incorrect because a flat mirror produces uniform reflections.

B is incorrect because a concave mirror, also called a converging mirror, causes beams of light to converge, or come together.

C is correct because a diverging mirror, also called a convex mirror, causes beams of light to spread apart and diverge.

D is incorrect because converging mirrors cause light to come together.

2. D

A is incorrect because line D is the imaginary perpendicular line used to measure the angle at which the ray hits the mirror. The mirror is represented by label B.

B is incorrect because the angle of reflected light is represented by line E.

C is incorrect because the angle at which light hits the mirror is represented by line C.

D is correct because line D shows the imaginary line in reference to which the angles of light are measured; this line is perpendicular to a surface at the point the ray intersects the surface.

3. B

A is incorrect because convex mirrors are diverging mirrors. They can be used to show a large area.

B is correct because convex mirrors are diverging mirrors. They allow one person to observe a large area of the store from one position.

C is incorrect because the described mirror is a diverging mirror, but it would not be used to produce a bright beam of light. Producing beams of light is a function of converging mirrors.

D is incorrect because a convex mirror is a diverging mirror, not a converging mirror.

4. C

A is incorrect because a flat lens would not spread out beams of light in such a way as to focus faraway objects.

B is incorrect because a convex lens is used to magnify images and is most often used to correct vision problems like farsightedness.

C is correct because a diverging lens spreads out beams of light and makes images at a distance more focused.

D is incorrect because a converging lens is used to correct vision problems like farsightedness. Converging lenses are most often used to magnify close-up images.

5. B

A is incorrect because light reflects off a mirror according to the law of reflection.

B is correct because the light will reflect at the same size angle at which it hits the mirror. A ray of light that strikes the mirror at 45 degrees will reflect at 45 degrees.

C is incorrect because the law of reflection states that the angle of reflection will equal the angle of incidence.

D is incorrect because light reflects uniformly off a mirror because a mirror is a smooth surface. Light reflects in different angles off rough surfaces.

Lesson 4 Quiz

1. C   4. C
2. B   5. D
3. A

1. C

A is incorrect because label A points to the pupil. The pupil brings light into the eye.

B is incorrect because label B points to the cornea. The cornea helps refract light.

C is correct because label C points to the lens. The lens is responsible for focusing light images onto the retina.

D is incorrect because label D points to the retina.

2. B

A is incorrect because farsighted eyes cannot see things up close clearly. To correct this vision problem, the curve of the cornea can be increased (either with contacts or surgery).

B is correct because nearsighted eyes cannot see distances clearly, due to the fact that the image hits in front of the retina. This problem can be corrected by flattening the cornea so that the image from the lens hits the retina.

C is incorrect because most likely the retina is functioning correctly. The problem is most likely that the image is not hitting the retina but rather in front of the retina.

D is incorrect because the condition of not seeing objects clearly up close is also called farsightedness. Farsighted eyes can be corrected by increasing the curve of the cornea, not flattening it.

3. A

A is correct because rod cells are specialized cells located in the retina used for detecting low levels of light.

B is incorrect because cone cells are specialized cells for detecting daytime light levels and colors.

C is incorrect because blood cells are not a type of specialized eye cell.

D is incorrect because stem cells are not a type of specialized eye cell.

4. C

A is incorrect because our perception of depth and distance relies on our brain interpreting images from both eyes.

B is incorrect because our perception of depth and distance relies on our brain interpreting images from both eyes.

C is correct because depth perception and the sense of distance rely on our brain combining images from both eyes. Because the eyes are in different locations on the head, they see slightly different images.

D is incorrect because both eyes can see objects up close and at a distance. The slightly different position of each eye helps us perceive distance.

5. D

A is incorrect because eyes that cannot see clearly at any distance likely have a problem more serious than nearsightedness or farsightedness, such as cataracts.

B is incorrect because eyes that can see things clearly up close are nearsighted.

C is incorrect because eyes that cannot see clearly at a distance are nearsighted.

D is correct because farsighted eyes can see most clearly at a distance.

Lesson 5 Quiz

1. D   4. B
2. A   5. D
3. A

1. D

A is incorrect because eyeglasses control the way light reaches our retina; they don't carry information.

B is incorrect because neon lights are an example of visible light; they are not a method of transmitting information.

C is incorrect because a laser welder is used to control the way energy affects matter, not transmit information.

D is correct because a bar code scanner can transmit information, such as price, via light.

2. A

A is correct because candles use fire to produce light and fire, the oldest light technology, was used by ancient peoples.

B is incorrect because fire, and the controlled use of it, occurred well before people developed LEDs.

C is incorrect because fire, and the controlled use of it, occurred well before people developed fluorescent lighting.

D is incorrect because fire, and the controlled use of it, occurred well before people developed incandescent lighting.

3. A

A is correct because binoculars magnify objects that are too

far away to see clearly with the unaided eye.

B is incorrect because microscopes are used to magnify objects that are too small to see; the scientist's problem is that the owls are too far away.

C is incorrect because a laser scanner is used to access information about materials by utilizing light's ability to interact with matter; the scientist's problem is that the owls are too far away.

D is incorrect because an LED screen would be useful for displaying information, but a different tool is needed to observe animals from a distance.

4. B

A is incorrect because light that is produced when one color is concentrated and amplified is a property of laser, not incandescent, light.

B is correct because incandescent light is produced when material within the light becomes hot enough to produce visible radiation.

C is incorrect because fluorescent light is produced when gases that emit UV light are energized by an electric current; the UV light interacts with the phosphor coating in the bulb and is converted to visible light.

D is incorrect because light that is produced when solid materials are energized by electric currents is LED light.

5. D

A   is incorrect because the image shows a fiber optic cable, not a laser.

B   is incorrect because the image shows a fiber optic cable, not a LED screen.

C   is incorrect because the image shows a fiber optic cable, not a fluorescent light.

D   is correct because the image shows a fiber optic cable. Fiber optic cables can bend and fit in tight spaces, making them suitable for moving light through small openings.

Lesson 1 Alternative Assessment

EM at Home: Poster shows electromagnetic waves and their wavelength, and how they are used at home, in school, in health care, and other settings.

Light and Stars: Diagram or illustration shows how scientists have used their understanding of light to determine whether stars are moving toward or away from Earth.

A Colorful Performance: Skit explains how the color of visible light is related to its wavelength.

Found Prisms: Presentations show how the prism works and explains the differences among the colors that one sees.

Make a Table: Tables list all waves of the EM spectrum in order of increasing or decreasing wave-length or frequency.

Concept Map: Concept map relates to the electromagnetic spectrum, and uses words and images to express ideas and concepts that are important to understand.

Lesson 2 Alternative Assessment

Vocabulary: Story tells what happens to a group of light beams that leave the sun, enter Earth's atmosphere, and interact with different media, such as water and grass.

Examples: Lists include three examples of objects that reflect light, three objects that scatter light, and three objects that do not transmit light. Characteristics common to each group are listed.

Analysis: Explanation describes why a white shirt glows a brilliant purple when lit with ultraviolet light.

Observations: Observations note discuss the way the pencil looks bent in the water and explain why the pencil looks this way.

Details: Work explains why a single lamp can light a whole room, and what happens to the light when it encounters a glass of water, a metal filing cabinet, and a filmy window curtain.

Lesson 3 Alternative Assessment

Plane Mirrors: Presentation focuses on flat mirrors that form virtual images that are reversed left to right.

Concave Mirrors: Presentation focuses on converging mirrors that form a real image that is smaller than the object being viewed, or a virtual image that is larger than the object being viewed.

Convex Mirrors: Presentation focuses on diverging mirrors that form a virtual image that is smaller than the object being viewed.

Convex Lenses: Presentation focuses on converging lens that form a virtual image that is larger or a real image that is smaller than the object being viewed.

Concave Lenses: Presentation focuses on diverging lens that forms a virtual image that is smaller than the object being viewed.

Lesson 4 Alternative Assessment

The entire process of vision is described or illustrated, from light entering the eye, to the image being transferred to the retina, to the impulses being sent to the brain for processing. Common vision problems and their solutions are discussed and detailed.

Lesson 5 Alternative Assessment

Comparing: Sketches should show how a laser light is different from the light beam of a flashlight.

Name a Tool: Paragraphs should name one optical tool, describe how it works, and explain how it is used.

Identifying Relationships: Venn Diagrams should compare LED and fluorescent light bulbs.

Draw a Poster: Posters should explain the concept of total internal reflection.

Doppler Radar: Weather reports for your town should include the use of Doppler radar.

Calculate Distance: Sketches should show how the speed of light and a laser beam be used to measure the distance between two satellites.

Lasers and Nanotechnology: Multimedia or oral presentations should explore how lasers are having a big impact on nanotechnology.

Design a Pinhole Camera: Designs should list the materials need, include the steps for how to put the camera together, and explain how the camera will take pictures.

Performance-Based Assessment

See Unit 3, Lesson 1

2. The regions should be arranged from left to right: radiowaves → microwaves → infrared → visible light → ultraviolet → X-rays → gamma rays

3. Wavelength decreases from left to right. The longest wavelengths are found in the radiowave region, while the shortest wavelengths are found in the gamma ray region.

4. Frequency increases from left to right. The lowest frequencies are found in the radiowave region, while the highest frequencies are found in the gamma ray region.

5. The widths of the sections indicate the span of wavelengths/frequencies covered in that region. The visible region covers the smallest span of wavelengths within the electromagnetic spectrum.

6. Humans can detect visible light with their eyes and infrared radiation through their ability to sense heat.

Unit Review

Vocabulary

1. T See Unit 3, Lesson 2
2. T See Unit 3, Lesson 5
3. F See Unit 3, Lesson 1
4. T See Unit 3, Lesson 2
5. T See Unit 3, Lesson 2

Key Concepts

6. C	9. B	12. B
7. C	10. A	13. D
8. A	11. C	

6. C See Unit 3, Lesson 4

A   is incorrect because the human eye can only see wavelengths in the visible spectrum.

B   is incorrect because the sun emits electromagnetic waves that the eyes and brain do not rely on to see color.

C   is correct because the eye detects various wavelengths of light and sends the information to the brain, which interprets them as colors.

D   is incorrect because human eyes detect wavelengths of light that are reflected by surfaces as well, and light waves don't necessarily need a medium to travel.

7. C See Unit 3, Lesson 4

A   is incorrect because neither part of the eye is a type of cell but the cornea and retina are made up of cells.

B   is incorrect because the lens is not a cell but an eye part that helps focus light rays.

C   is correct because rod cells detect low levels of light and cone cells help detect colors in brighter light.

D   is incorrect because the cornea is not a type of cell.

8. A See Unit 3, Lesson 1

A   is correct because the wavelengths listed in the column increase in frequency from the lowest, radio waves, to the highest, ultraviolet.

B   is incorrect because the list does not go in order from lowest to highest frequency.

C   is incorrect because laser light is not a wavelength on its own in the spectrum.

D   is incorrect because the list does not go in order from lowest to highest frequency.

9. B See Unit 3, Lesson 2

A   is incorrect because it only lists a few sources of light.

B   is correct because matter can reflect, refract, or absorb light.

C   incorrect because laser light is not a wavelength on its own and what wavelengths of light go through matter depends on the optical properties of the matter.

D   is incorrect because matter does not necessarily change

only the frequency and wavelength of light waves.

10. A See Unit 3, Lesson 2

A is correct because the yellow light passes through the glass, but the red light does not.

B is incorrect because the yellow light passes through the glass, but the red light does not.

C incorrect because the diagram does not show either red or yellow light being reflected by the glass.

D is incorrect because only yellow light is passing through the glass.

11. C See Unit 3, Lesson 3

A is incorrect because the diagram shows the exact path of a ray of light and not scattering.

B is incorrect because the normal is an imaginary line and cannot absorb light.

C is correct because the normal is an imaginary line perpendicular to the surface that is used to measure the angles of incoming and outgoing light rays.

D is incorrect because the normal is not dependant on the angle of the incoming ray, it is always perpendicular to the surface being struck.

12. B See Unit 3, Lesson 2

A is incorrect because the liquid in glass A did not absorb light, it transmitted light.

B is correct because the light was transmitted by the transparent liquid in glass A

and scattered by the translucent liquid in B.

C is incorrect because the liquid in glass A is not translucent and the liquid in B is not transparent.

D is incorrect because the light was transmitted through the liquid in glass A and was not scattered by it.

13. D See Unit 3, Lesson 1

A is incorrect because frequency does not determine the speed of electromagnetic waves.

B is incorrect because frequency does not determine the speed of electromagnetic waves.

C is incorrect because infrared and ultraviolet waves travel at the same speed.

D is correct because all electromagnetic waves travel at the speed of light.

Critical Thinking
14. See Unit 3, Lesson 4

- The cornea is a transparent part at the front of the eyeball that allows light to enter.

- Light is refracted after it enters the cornea.

- The retina lines the inside back areas of the eye.

- Light comes to a focus on the retina and cells in the retina help detect and transmit signals to the brain.

15. See Unit 3, Lesson 3

- flat, convex, concave

- A converging mirror has a concave shape and causes a

parallel beam of light to converge, or come together. A diverging mirror has a convex shape and causes a parallel beam of light to diverge, or spread apart.

- A real image forms where light from the object converges and actually passes through the image. A real image forms from a real focus in front of a concave mirror. A virtual image is an image from which light appears to diverge. A virtual image seems to be behind a flat mirror.

- Converging lenses are used for magnifying mirrors, telescopes, microscopes, binoculars, cameras, and projectors.

Connect Essential Questions
16. See Unit 3, Lesson 1, Lesson 4 and Lesson 5

- Light comes from the sun, from fire, from light bulbs, and from all objects hot enough to glow.

- Visible light is a form of electromagnetic radiation and all electromagnetic radiation travels as waves along electric and magnetic fields. Energy from the sun reaches Earth because light waves do not need to move in a medium and can travel across the near vacuum of space.

- burning candles, incandescent lights, fluorescent lights, LEDs, and lasers

- Fire from burning materials, such as candlewicks, give off heat and light. Incandescent light comes from material that is hot enough to glow, or produce radiation that is visible. Fluorescent lights contain gases that give off light when an electric current passes through the gases. LEDs, or light-emitting diodes, contain solid materials that give off light when an electric current passes through the solids.

Unit Test A

Key Concepts

1. D	5. A	9. B
2. A	6. A	10. B
3. B	7. C	11. C
4. C	8. D	12. C

1. D

A is incorrect because the pupil, together with the iris, controls how much light enters the eye.

B is incorrect because the cornea helps refract and focus light as it enters the eye.

C is incorrect because rod cells help us distinguish things in low-light situations.

D is correct because cone cells are responsible for daytime seeing, including distinguishing colors.

2. A

A is correct because LEDs emit light when solid particles within the lights are energized with an electric current.

B is incorrect because lasers emit light by concentrating and amplifying small wavelengths of light.

C is incorrect because incandescent lights emit light when material within the light becomes hot enough to produce visible radiation.

D is incorrect because LEDs emit light when solid particles within the lights are energized with an electric current.

3. B

A is incorrect because each of the viewers will see the image, as shown by label X.

B is correct because the image appears to be coming from behind the mirror. As the rays are extended in straight lines from the eyes of the viewers, the image is formed where the lines intersect. In this case, the image is behind the mirror.

C is incorrect because each viewer will see the same image. The angle will be slightly different for each viewer, but they will all be viewing the same image, X.

D is incorrect because in the diagram above, X is behind the mirror.

4. C

A is incorrect because eyeglasses do not store light.

B is incorrect because eyeglasses do change the way light enters the eye, but they do not store or transmit information.

C is correct because lenses, such as those found in eyeglasses, allow us to control the way we see light.

D is incorrect because eyeglasses do not emit light.

5. A

A is correct because the longest wavelengths of light refract the least. Of the colors listed, red has the longest wavelength.

B is incorrect because the shortest wavelengths of light refract the most. Color 1 refracts the least, so it cannot be blue light.

C is incorrect because the longest wavelengths of light refract the least. Color 1 could not be green light because the wavelength of green light is shorter than the wavelength of red light.

D is incorrect because the longest wavelengths of light refract the least. Color 1 could not be yellow light because the wavelength of yellow light is shorter than the wavelength of red light.

6. A

A is correct because parallel beams of light, when striking a converging mirror, will all converge at a focal point.

B is incorrect because parallel beams will not reflect back as parallel beams when they strike a converging mirror. However, a beam of light shining from the focal point will create a parallel beam.

C is incorrect because beams that spread out after hitting a mirror occur with diverging mirrors, not converging mirrors.

D is incorrect because the focal point is in front of, not behind, the mirror. Parallel beams of light will all reflect to a focal point.

7. C

A is incorrect because an opaque material does not transmit any light at all.

B is incorrect because fog, while it is somewhat reflective, is best described as translucent.

C is correct because only blurry images can be seen through fog.

D is incorrect because it is not possible to see clearly through fog.

8. D

A is incorrect because enlarging the pupil is not used to correct vision problems; also, contact lenses can be used to correct both types of vision problems.

B is incorrect because contact lenses can be used to correct both types of vision problems.

C is incorrect because enlarging the pupil is not used to correct vision problems.

D is correct because flattening the cornea can correct nearsightedness and help refocus light on the retina; also, converging lenses are used to correct farsightedness by focusing light images inward toward the retina, correcting the problem of

images falling behind the retina.

9. B

A is incorrect because images can be either virtual or real, depending on the location of the object relative to the focal point of the lens or mirror.

B is correct because reflected images can be larger or smaller, real or virtual, upright or inverted, or at different locations from the object.

C is incorrect because though images and objects can appear to be different sizes, this is not always the case, so this statement is not true.

D is incorrect because though some images do look exactly like the object, this is not always the case, and so the statement is not true.

10. B

A is incorrect because, among the choices, the graph shows that x-rays, not radio waves, have the shortest wavelength and therefore have the highest frequency.

B is correct because, among the choices, the graph shows that x-rays have the shortest wavelength and therefore have the highest frequency.

C is incorrect because, among the choices, the graph shows that x-rays, not infrared waves, have the shortest wavelength and therefore have the highest frequency.

D is incorrect because, among the choices, the graph shows

that x-rays, not ultraviolet waves, have the shortest wavelength and therefore have the highest frequency.

11. C

A is incorrect because our eyes blink constantly. This characteristic of eyes does not significantly impact the transmittal of messages to the brain.

B is incorrect because the retina does not interpret the images, the brain does.

C is correct because once images are in the retina, they are transmitted to the brain via the optic nerve.

D is incorrect because light moves from the cornea to the retina, not the other way around.

12. C

A is incorrect because electromagnetic waves travel along magnetic fields, but magnetic fields are not electromagnetic radiation.

B is incorrect because sound waves are not electromagnetic.

C is correct because the transfer of energy as electromagnetic waves is called electromagnetic radiation.

D is incorrect because electromagnetic waves do not need a medium in order to travel.

Critical Thinking

13.

- higher frequency = shorter wavelength

- lower frequency = longer wavelength

- frequency and wavelength = inversely related

Extended Response

14.

- a description of how the backpack would appear through red glass and an explanation of why (e.g., *The backpack would appear red through red glass because the glass transmits only red light*; etc.)

- a description of how the backpack would appear through blue glass and an explanation of why (e.g., *The backpack would appear black through the blue glass because the glass transmits only blue light*; etc.)

Unit Test B

Key Concepts

1. A	5. A	9. B
2. C	6. C	10. B
3. B	7. A	11. C
4. A	8. D	12. C

1. A

A is correct because cone cells are specialized cells in the retina that help us perceive colors.

B is incorrect because our brain, working in conjunction with both eyes, helps us perceive distance.

C is incorrect because cone cells detect daytime levels of light and distinguish color, they do not reflect light.

D is incorrect because rod cells, not cone cells, are important for low-light levels.

2. C

A is incorrect because LEDs emit light by energizing solid materials within the light, not because of heat; in contrast, fluorescent light is produced when gases that emit UV light are energized by an electric current; the UV light interacts with the phosphor coating in the bulb and is converted to visible light.

B is incorrect because LED lights emit light by energizing solid materials within the light, while fluorescent light is produced when gases that emit UV light are energized by an electric current; the UV light interacts with the phosphor coating in the bulb and is converted to visible light. Light that is produced by concentrating wavelengths is laser light; light produced by heat is incandescent light.

C is correct because LED lights emit light by energizing solid materials within the light, while fluorescent light is produced when gases that emit UV light are energized by an electric current; the UV light interacts with the phosphor coating in the bulb and is converted to visible light.

D is incorrect because LED lights emit light by energizing solid materials, not gases, within the light; in contrast, fluorescent light is produced when gases that emit UV light are energized by an electric current; the UV light interacts with the phosphor coating in the bulb and is converted to visible light, not by concentrating wavelengths.

3. B

A is incorrect because flat mirrors produce virtual images, not real images.

B is correct because an image is formed where rays of an object intersect. In the diagram, the rays must be extended backward to see the image, so the image appears to be behind the mirror. The image is not really behind the image, and light does actually pass through the image, so it is a virtual image.

C is incorrect because the X depicts an image only, not a magnified image.

D is incorrect because two different viewers are viewing one object. Where the rays intersect is where the image of the object is located, not images of the viewers (though it would be possible for the viewers to see each other in the mirror as well as the object).

4. A

A is correct because the sunlight's energy physically changes the food as it cooks.

B is incorrect because the focused light does not physically change the object that is magnified.

C is incorrect because the optical fibers transmit pulses of light, not physical matter.

D is incorrect because corrective lenses change the angle at which light enters the eyes, but they do not change physical matter.

5. A

A is correct because the longest wavelengths of light refract the least. Of the colors listed, red has the longest wavelength.

B is incorrect because though red would be a correct color for Color 1, the explanation is that red refracts the least, not the most. Longer wavelengths, such as red, refract the least.

C is incorrect because Color 1 is more likely to be red than blue. Red is a longer wavelength of color, and therefore refracts the least.

D is incorrect because Color 1 is more likely to be red than blue. Red is a longer wavelength of color, and therefore refracts the least.

6. C

A is incorrect because a beam of light placed at the focal point of a converging mirror will reflect off the mirror and form a parallel beam of light.

B is incorrect because light that diverges is a characteristic of diverging mirrors, not converging mirrors.

C is correct because a beam of light placed at the focal point of a converging mirror will

first shine toward the mirror. It will reflect off the mirror and, because of the curvature of the mirror, will form a parallel beam of light.

D is incorrect because converging mirrors do have a focal point that is in front of the mirror. Diverging mirrors have focal points that appear to be behind the mirror.

7. A

A is correct because only blurry images can be seen through fog, so the fog is translucent. Translucent materials scatter light.

B is incorrect because an opaque material does not transmit any light at all, and some images are visible through fog.

C is incorrect because fog is somewhat reflective, but it is best described as translucent. Translucent materials scatter light.

D is incorrect because people cannot see clearly through fog.

8. D

A is incorrect because enlarging the pupil is not used to correct vision problems; also, contact lenses can be used to correct both types of vision problems.

B is incorrect because contact lenses can be used to correct both types of vision problems.

C is incorrect because enlarging the pupil is not used to correct vision problems.

D is correct because increasing the curve of the cornea can correct farsightedness by refocusing light on the retina; also, diverging lenses are used to correct nearsightedness by refocusing light images so they no longer fall in front of the retina.

9. B

A is incorrect because the first position of the object would produce a real image, and the second position would produce a virtual image.

B is correct because the first position of the object would produce a real image, and the second position would produce a virtual image. An object placed farther than the focal point produces a real image, and an object placed nearer than the focal point produces a virtual image. This is true for concave mirrors only.

C is incorrect because the first position of the object would produce a real image, and the second position would produce a virtual image.

D is incorrect because the first position of the object would produce a real image, and the second position would produce a virtual image.

10. B

A is incorrect because, among the choices, the graph shows that x-rays, not radio waves, have the shortest wavelength.

B is correct because, among the choices, the graph shows that x-rays have the shortest wavelength.

C is incorrect because, among the choices, the graph shows that x-rays, not infrared waves, have the shortest wavelength.

D is incorrect because, among the choices, the graph shows that x-rays, not ultraviolet waves, have the shortest wavelength.

11. C

A is incorrect because before light images go to the brain (via the optic nerve), they must pass through the retina.

B is incorrect because light images move from the front of the eye to the back of the eye, and then on to the brain (via the optic nerve).

C is correct because light images move from the lens to the retina, and then on to the brain (via the optic nerve).

D is incorrect because the process is reversed; light images move from the lens to the retina, and then on to the brain (via the optic nerve).

12. C

A is incorrect because electromagnetic waves do not require a medium to transfer energy.

B is incorrect because a magnetic field is a region around magnetic material, not the transfer of energy as electromagnetic waves.

C is correct because electromagnetic radiation is the term to describe the transfer of energy as electromagnetic waves.

D is incorrect because wavelength and amplitude are features of waves, not the transfer of energy as waves.

Critical Thinking

13.

- higher frequency = shorter wavelength
- lower frequency = longer wavelength
- frequency and wavelength = inversely related
- frequency and energy = directly related

Extended Response

14.

- a description of how the backpack would appear through blue glass and an explanation of why (e.g., *The backpack would appear blue through blue glass because the glass transmits only blue light*; etc.)
- a description of how the backpack would appear through red glass and an explanation of why (e.g., *The backpack would appear black through the red glass because the glass transmits only red light*; etc.)

End-of-Module Test

1. C	11. A	21. C
2. C	12. A	22. D
3. A	13. B	23. A
4. C	14. C	24. D
5. C	15. D	25. C
6. B	16. A	26. D
7. C	17. C	27. B
8. B	18. D	28. B
9. C	19. C	29. C
10. B	20. B	30. D

1. C See Unit 1, Lesson 1

A is incorrect because the wave will continue to move through the water.

B is incorrect because mechanical waves move slower in liquids than they do in solids.

C is correct because mechanical waves move slower in liquids than they do in solids.

D is incorrect because the speed of a wave depends on the medium through which it travels, so the wave's speed will change when it reaches the water.

2. C See Unit 3, Lesson 3

A is incorrect because the object is in front of the mirror. It is the image of the object that seems to be behind the mirror.

B is incorrect because the viewers are in front of the mirror, as shown in the diagram.

C is correct because our brains interpret light in straight lines. The depth of the object, when reflected in the mirror, makes it look as though it's beyond, or behind, the mirror, though this is not indeed the case.

D is incorrect because the rays of the image are coming from the object, which is placed in front of, not behind, the mirror.

3. A See Unit 2, Lesson 2

A is correct because sound waves travel most quickly in a dense solid.

B   is incorrect because sound waves travel slowest in a gas.

C   is incorrect because sound waves travel faster in a solid than in a liquid.

D   is incorrect because sound waves travel more quickly in the denser solid rock.

4. C See Unit 2, Lesson 1

A   is incorrect because increased wavelength implies a lower pitch.

B   is incorrect because decreased frequency implies a lower pitch; also, the sound is quieter, not louder.

C   is correct because increased frequency implies a higher pitch and decreased amplitude implies a quieter sound.

D   is incorrect because increased amplitude implies a louder sound.

5. C See Unit 2, Lesson 1

A   is incorrect because more compressions imply a higher frequency, which is related to the sound source, not the medium.

B   is incorrect because an increase in the distance of points N and M implies a decrease in frequency, which is related to the sound source, not the medium.

C   is correct because solids have more particles within them then air, which is a gas.

D   is incorrect because sound waves can travel through solids.

6. B See Unit 3, Lesson 3

A   is incorrect because diverging lenses are usually concave on both sides. Converging lenses are usually convex.

B   is correct because converging lenses focus parallel beams of light to a focal point.

C   is incorrect because diverging lenses, not converging lenses, cause parallel beams of light to spread out.

D   is incorrect because diverging lenses, not converging lenses, are thinner at the center than at the edges.

7. C See Unit 3, Lesson 2

A   is incorrect because light scatters when it enters a translucent material. It does not bounce straight back.

B   is incorrect because light scatters when it enters a translucent material. It does not move straight through.

C   is correct because light scatters when it enters a translucent material. Spreading out in all directions is another way to describe scattering.

D   is incorrect because moving through but in a new direction is refraction. Light scatters, not refracts, when it enters a translucent material.

8. B See Unit 3, Lesson 5

A   is incorrect because a book may contain many images, but video is the term used to describe a sequence of images that captures motion data.

B   is correct because video is formed by a sequence of images. When the images are strung together and played back, the process creates the illusion of motion and continuity between the images.

C   is incorrect because a photo is only one image; video is the correct term for a sequence of images strung together to capture motion data.

D   is incorrect because computers can play videos, but a computer is not defined as a sequence of images strung together to capture motion data.

9. C See Unit 2, Lesson 1

A   is incorrect because Car C does not experience a Doppler effect, so it must be in the lead.

B   is incorrect because Car C does not experience a Doppler effect, so it must be in the lead.

C   is correct because Car C does not experience a Doppler effect, so it must be in the lead; Car B is second so the siren is increasing in pitch; and Car A is in front of Car C but not in the lead, so it is moving away from the siren.

D   is incorrect because Car B is moving toward the siren while Car A is moving away from it, so the Doppler effect would be reversed.

10. B See Unit 2, Lesson 3

A   is incorrect because a telephone's mouthpiece changes sound waves into electric signals.

B is correct because a telephone's mouthpiece changes sound waves into electric signals. These electric signals are transmitted to the receiving phone, which changes the electric signals back into sound waves that are heard through the earpiece.

C is incorrect because a telephone's mouthpiece changes sound waves into electric signals.

D is incorrect because a telephone's mouthpiece changes sound waves into electric signals.

11. A See Unit 1, Lesson 2

A is correct because mechanical waves move more quickly through a solid than through a gas.

B is incorrect because mechanical waves move more slowly in a gas than they do in a solid.

C is incorrect because mechanical waves change speed when they change media.

D is incorrect because the speed of mechanical waves remains the same in any particular medium.

12. A See Unit 1, Lesson 2

A is correct because a period is measured in time.

B is incorrect because speed is distance traveled in a given time.

C is incorrect because amplitude is a distance measurement.

D is incorrect because wavelength is a distance measurement.

13. B See Unit 1, Lesson 1

A is incorrect because a medium is the material through which a wave moves; it is not a type of wave.

B is correct because the particles are vibrating perpendicular to the direction of the wave motion.

C is incorrect because the particles would need to vibrate along the x-axis to be parallel to the direction of the wave motion and be considered a longitudinal wave.

D is incorrect because there is not enough information to conclude the wave is electromagnetic.

14. C See Unit 2, Lesson 2

A is incorrect because Brownian motion is the name for the motion of all matter.

B is incorrect because a tuned instrument is not a natural frequency but a human-made one.

C is correct because all objects have a natural frequency or set of frequencies at which they vibrate.

D is incorrect because the background noise of the universe is called background radiation.

15. D See Unit 1, Lesson 2

A is incorrect because their units are different; they cannot be added.

B is incorrect because speed does not have units of 1 / (time)(distance).

C is incorrect because speed does not have units of (distance)(time).

D is correct because speed has units of distance/time.

16. A See Unit 3, Lesson 2

A is correct because ray 1 travels through the material without reflecting or without being absorbed or scattered.

B is incorrect because ray 2 is absorbed; it does not travel through the material.

C is incorrect because ray 3 is scattered; it does not travel through the material.

D is incorrect because ray 4 is reflected; it does not travel through the material.

17. C See Unit 3, Lesson 4

A is incorrect because rod and cone cells are in the retina, not the brain. They help us see in low light, and they help us perceive color.

B is incorrect because our brains combine the two-dimensional images from both eyes.

C is correct because our brains combine the two-dimensional images from each eye to form a three-dimensional image. This occurs because each eye is in a slightly different position, so the images are different. The brain combines these two-dimensional images to help us gain depth perception and gauge distance.

D is incorrect because in normal eyes, both eyes work equally to perceive images.

18. D See Unit 3, Lesson 3

A is incorrect because flashlights use converging, not diverging, mirrors.

B is incorrect because telescopes use converging, not diverging, mirrors.

C is incorrect because a microscope uses converging, not diverging, mirrors.

D is correct because a mirror that shows details of a large area is a diverging mirror. A mirror used to show the details of a dangerous intersection is most likely to be a diverging mirror.

19. C See Unit 3, Lesson 4

A is incorrect because blindness cannot be corrected by flattening the cornea. In many instances, blindness cannot be corrected.

B is incorrect because farsightedness can be corrected by increasing the curve of the cornea, not flattening it.

C is correct because nearsightedness can be corrected by flattening the cornea. This changes the way light enters the eye and allows the eye to more clearly see things at a distance.

D is incorrect because color vision deficiency cannot be corrected.

20. B See Unit 2, Lesson 2

A is incorrect because the Doppler effect requires the source of sound to be moving toward or moving away from the listener.

B is correct because the sound waves are reflecting off the smooth surface, producing echoes.

C is incorrect because resonance happens when a sound wave matches the natural frequency of another object and causes it to vibrate.

D is incorrect because distance and time are not indicated in the diagram.

21. C See Unit 2, Lesson 2

A is incorrect because air particles are not destroyed during a sonic boom.

B is incorrect because a sonic boom is a shock wave from the convergence of many sound waves.

C is correct because a sonic boom is a shock wave from the convergence of many sound waves.

D is incorrect because a sonic boom always occurs after the sound barrier is broken.

22. D See Unit 3, Lesson 1

A is incorrect because the energy of an electromagnetic wave does not affect its ability to reach Earth.

B is incorrect because the frequency of an electromagnetic wave does not affect its ability to reach Earth.

C is incorrect because the wavelength of an electromagnetic wave does not affect its ability to reach Earth.

D is correct because, in order to travel through outer space (a vacuum), electromagnetic waves must be able to travel without a medium.

23. A See Unit 3, Lesson 1

A is correct because the statement is true. The graph shows that gamma rays are shorter than x-ray waves.

B is incorrect because the statement is false. The graph shows that ultraviolet waves are shorter, not longer, than radio waves.

C is incorrect because the statement is false. The graph shows that visible light waves are shorter, not longer, than microwaves.

D is incorrect because the statement is false. The graph shows that infrared waves are longer, not shorter, than ultraviolet waves.

24. D See Unit 1, Lesson 1

A is incorrect because waves do not transfer matter (the jellyfish) from one place to another.

B is incorrect because waves do not transfer matter (the jellyfish) from one place to another.

C is incorrect because waves cause matter (the jellyfish) to move up and down.

D is correct because waves cause matter (the jellyfish) to

move around its original position, but the matter's particles return to their original position after the wave is gone.

25. C See Unit 2, Lesson 3

A is incorrect because if the signals were reflecting off of objects above the ocean floor, the signals would reach the submarine more quickly.

B is incorrect because this does not account for the change in signal timing.

C is correct because longer times for reflections indicate an increase in distance from the ocean floor.

D is incorrect because longer times for reflections indicate an increase, not a decrease, in distance from the ocean floor.

26. D See Unit 3, Lesson 4

A is incorrect because label A points to the pupil. The pupil works in conjunction with the iris to change shape under varying light conditions.

B is incorrect because label B points to the cornea. The cornea helps refract light.

C is incorrect because label C points to the lens. The lens is responsible for focusing light images onto the retina.

D is correct because label D points to the retina. The retina is where light images are received from the lens before being transmitted to the brain, and it contains specialized cells called rods and cones.

27. B See Unit 3, Lesson 1

A is incorrect because to the human eye, the lowest frequency appears red, not green, and the highest frequency appears violet, not red.

B is correct because to the human eye, the lowest frequency appears red, and the highest frequency appears violet.

C is incorrect because to the human eye, the lowest frequency appears red, not blue, and the highest frequency appears violet, not orange.

D is incorrect because to the human eye, the lowest frequency appears red, not yellow, and the highest frequency appears violet, not green.

28. B See Unit 3, Lesson 2

A is incorrect because a banana does not produce its own light.

B is correct because the color of an opaque object, such as a banana, is the color it reflects.

C is incorrect because the color of an opaque object, such as a banana, is the color it reflects, not the color it absorbs.

D is incorrect because an opaque object, such as a banana, does not transmit light.

29. C See Unit 3, Lesson 5

A is incorrect because lasers produce light by concentrating and amplifying a limited wavelength.

B is incorrect because fiber optic cables don't produce light; they transmit light.

C is correct because fluorescent light is produced when gases that emit UV light are energized by an electric current; the UV light interacts with the phosphor coating in the bulb and is converted to visible light.

D is incorrect because incandescent lights produce light when material within the light becomes hot enough to produce visible radiation.

30. D See Unit 3, Lesson 5

A is incorrect because the image shows a fiber optic cable, not an incandescent light.

B is incorrect because the image shows a fiber optic cable, not a laser.

C is incorrect because the image shows a fiber optic cable, not a light-emitting diode.

D is correct because the image shows a fiber optic cable. Because the cables are small, flexible, and can carry light with little loss, they are beneficial to the medical field. One use includes sending cables into a patient's body to illuminate it or to collect images.